TEACHER EDUCATION

TEACHER EDUCATION

Mohit Chakrabarti

ISBN : 978-93-5128-051-4

Price : ₹ 675

Third Edition, 2014

Published by

Kalpaz Publications
C-30, Satyawati Nagar,
Delhi – 110052
E-mail: kalpaz@hotmail.com
Ph.: 9212142040

Laser Typesetting: Gyan Print (AB-I)
Printed at: G. Print Process, Delhi

Cataloging in Publication Data—DK
Courtesy: D.K. Agencies (P) Ltd. <docinfo@dkagencies.com>

Chakrabarti, Mohit, 1941-
Teacher education / Mohit Chakrabarti. -- 3rd ed.
p. cm.
Includes bibliographical references.
ISBN 9789351280514

1. Teachers--Training of. 2. Teachers--Training of--India.
3. Education--Philosophy. 4. Education--India--Philosophy.
I. Title.

DDC 370.711 23

Dedicated to

Professor N.B. Biswas

Dean, Asutosh Mukhopadhaya School of Education,

Assam University, Silchar

and

Professor R.P. Vadhera

Director, UGC, Academic Staff College

Mizoram University, Mizoram

Contents

Preface

Education today is under critical scanner. Teacher education, in particular, is now untiringly exploring new horizons in its diverse angles of vision and experimentation. While a vast arena of education and experiences pose multi-dimensional avenues of issues and perspectives in order to arrive at a crucial juncture in eliminating numerous constraints either in theories or in practices whatsoever or howsoever right from early childhood to the higher stages, the problems of continually frustrating outcome in having enriched the quality and splendid excellence are aggravating the whole citadel of education in general and teacher education in particular.

Despite the fact that much has been thought of and done in redefining and reframing the curriculum almost at every stage right from school to higher education, neither the institutions nor the parents and guardians belonging to heterogeneous sections of a pluralistic society in our vast country are at all happy for what is going on in the name of education and teaching. In fact, the twenty-first century expectations and priorities in teacher education are yet to encompass and negotiate some of the crucial issues in teacher education where the role of the teacher is yet to be clarified in terms of the mission, vision, goals and objectives in clear and distinct, pinpointed and easily accessible terms. Moreover, a sudden switchover from one framework to the other in overhauling the entire programme of action without undergoing the evaluation of the earlier one from all important and essential ends-in-view has already presented us with confusions worse confounded by enlarging the domain of undesirable ukase. Meanwhile, quality and excellence in teacher education are posing newer challenges. "Quality Enrichment in teacher Education" is a critical and in-depth study in this direction.

Teacher education in the twenty-first century calls forth quality to be properly and appropriately assessed from diverse dimensions. As any institution is always eager for its actual line of advancement in teaching-learning in terms of assessments from various standpoints, particularly from aesthetic perspectives, "Post-Accreditation Strategies for Quality Sustenance in Teacher Education: Aesthetic Parameters" might be a significant pointer in this direction.

That teacher education in the twenty-first century greatly pines for re-thinking and re-exploring the practical, useful and living educational programmes of action as Mahatma Gandhi introduced through Basic Education may very well be re-defined in our curriculum framework. "Teaching in the twenty-first century: Gandhian Guidelines" may serve this invaluable end-in-view.

Quite unhappily, teacher education and inter-relativity between educational process and environment are at crossroads with quality and excellence at present. "Teacher Education and Inter-relativity between Educational Process and Environment" is an intensive study on some of the crucial issues in this connection.

"Teacher Education and School Internship: A Quest for Quality Enrichment" and "Teacher Education for Professional Development of Teacher Educators" unfold some fundamental issues encompassing new horizons of teacher education.

"Teacher Education and the Individual Learner: Setting New Agenda for Negotiating Needs" might provoke the probing thoughts of anyone interested in teacher education for quality and excellence.

The educational philosophy of Swami Vivekananda holds the key to dynamic and positive education where the role of the teacher is to enable every learner to manifest the inherent perfection as best as possible. As one of the most vibrant and practical thinkers in education for fullness, his viewpoints and suggestions on the role of the teacher in inspiring and disseminating how to foster advancement of quality and excellence in education are very important especially in the context of the twenty-first century scenario in the arena of teacher education. "Vibrant Teacher Education: Vivekananda's Viewpoints" is a critical study on some of the most essential components contributing to better teacher education as Vivekananda has envisioned.

"Teacher Education and the Evolving Teacher: Sri Aurobindo's Guidelines" might attract the revered attention of all interested in the role of the evolving teacher in the twenty-first century.

I do hope and trust that "Teacher Education and Education for Cultural Development: Exploring Dynamic Avenues of Efflorescence" would add a new dimension to teacher education in the twenty-first century.

"Teacher Education and Reflective Teaching" and "Teacher Education and Tutoring" might bring forth a welcome change in Teacher Education and might reward me with pregnant suggestions from revered readers.

I gratefully recall some of the glorious moments of my discussions on teacher education with Professor N.B. Biswas, Dean, Asutosh Mukhopadaya School of Education, Assam University, Silchar and with Professor R.P. Vadhera, Director, UGC Academic Staff College, Mizoram University, who are sincerely contributing to quality and excellence in education. I humbly dedicate my book to them as a token of my reverence.

I would like to express my love, affection and best wishes to Sobdo and Priyanka, my son and daughter-in-law, who have extended their untiring cooperation in computer work.

If the book appeals to anyone interested in teacher education and rewards me with their apposite comments and suggestions, I would murmur within: "Go ahead with the love and blessings of all!"

Mohit Chakrabarti

Seemantika,
Seemanto Palli,
Santiniketan-731 235
West Bengal

1 Quality Enrichment in Teacher Education

Education is a thrilling and challenging activity. Teacher education is a more thrilling and challenging one because it is essentially concerned with two very crucial components—quality and excellence. The more is the quality, the greater is the excellence turning knowledge into wisdom, accuracy into poignancy, integrity into serenity, and coherence into resonance in contemplation and action. It is, therefore, universally agreed that where education is a success, teacher education takes the role of a true task master, an architect of architects, the teachers as we modestly respect them.

Teacher education today is really concerned with quality and excellence. At least five very emerging, critical, difficult and challenging components serve as stimulants and spurts in teacher education for acceleration of quality and excellence. These are motivation, positive thinking, attention, intelligence and exercise. While motivation makes inroads to inward excellence, positive thinking and attention serve as pillars and protectors of motivation. Intelligence and exercise make all educational processes and procedures normal and smooth, advancing and effective.

The history of teacher education in our country right now is not very bright and positive. Promises are hardly kept and procedures fight shy of the desirable span of solidarity. While tall and epigrammatic statements like the destiny of the country resting on the classrooms holds high on the altar of teaching and learning, it is equally interesting that quality and excellence in teaching are still lagging behind. As a result, teaching is yet to become a really meaningful and living reality.

The seven-fold factor in teaching learning viz., knowledge, understanding, skill, interest, attitude, aptitude and appreciation necessitates coherence and consolidation at every stage in education. For such consolidation and coherence, the teacher's main role is to translate quality and excellence in terms of all these essential factors. Mere accumulation of knowledge and acceleration of understanding eat away all the vital elements of learning, where the teacher has the habitual proneness to while away the most precious moments of teaching in drilling and mechanical teaching. Again, knowledge lost in bare storage of understanding and information makes both teaching and learning dead and sterile. Unfortunately, the quality and the excellence of a teacher are even now evaluated more or less in terms of dissemination of the above without having any reference to pupil illumination in qualitative and reflective thinking and experimentations.

Skillful and interesting teaching, attitude-savvy and aptitude-building motivation, enabling learners to bank judicially upon self-appreciation and self-decision—these are some of the fundamental characteristics of teaching learning. If education is directed towards self-education from the right perspectives of quality and excellence in teaching-learning, the joy of both teaching and learning becomes a living and pulsating reality.

A radical and innovative curriculum in teacher education with real professional and humane teaching as the fundamental end-in-view of advancement in quality and excellence is the need of the hour. This is why a major paradigm-shift from the age-old practice on some psychological aspects in child education without caring for contextual components of a process-based pattern of scientific, objective, pinpointed, creative, critical, judicious and reflective teaching in an ardent ambience of socio-cultural, aesthetic and political contexts of the learner will ensure desirable quality and excellence. The experience, observation and consolidation in theoretical in-depth in teaching-learning ought to bring about a change in bookish teaching-learning in order to ensure the fact that quality and excellence never rest on acquired knowledge but on the conceptual knowledge generated, nurtured, cultured and illumined with an unending and sustained adventure in personal and social involvements where the teacher and the learner are inseparable partners in the generation of knowledge.

A genuine pursuit in the deeper discussions and reflections in an enviable climate of consciousness in self-study, self-development and self-enrichment in teaching and learning ought to be given a warm and free welcome in the arena of teacher education where structured and stereotyped assignments still dominate. It is time to take immediate action to eliminate given knowledge, given theories, teacher-directed activities and shift our attention to self-study, self-development and self-enrichment for excellence in teacher education.

Teacher education is a complex activity. This becomes all the more complex because whatever education is imparted during the short period of its span of activities needs a change right now. Short training in education now is no training in the clear sense that it fails to ignite quality and excellence inherent in both the teacher and the learner. A longer duration of professional education as teacher education rightly necessitates will certainly make ample room for integration with other disciplines encompassing humanities, arts and liberal sciences.

The importance of school internship in teacher education is undeniable. This not only allows the teacher-learner to explore newer avenues of quality enrichment but also promises a healthy and disciplined climate of teaching-leaning. The institution, as it were, becomes the altar of advancement in education where joy and freedom, creativity and spontaneity, sympathy and empathy become the hallmark of quality education. Reflections on the practice of teaching as it more often than not remain absent from our assignments become living and interesting, loving and stimulating for excellence and ascent.

The role of quality enriched teachers in education is undeniable. Parents are fed up with money-spinning education. Society is insensitive to teaching and learning where teaching in most cases has lost the avenues of excellence and advancement, and learning, ironically, has lost its initial 'I' in the attraction and aggravation of earning through a pale and passive passport. The National Curriculum Framework (NCF) 2005 with which the present contributor was closely associated and the National Curriculum Framework for Teacher Education (NCFTE) 2009 where, too, the present contributor was deeply involved, have intensively sorted out and disseminated most of the essential quality pointers to become vibrant teachers of the twenty-first century. As the NCFTE 2009 strongly advocates:

> The importance of competent teachers to the nation's school system can in no way be overemphasised. It is well-known that the quality and extent of learner achievement are determined primarily by teacher competence, sensitivity and teacher motivation. It is common knowledge too that the academic and professional standards of teachers constitute a critical component of essential learning conditions for achieving the educational goals. The length of academic preparation, the level and quality of subject-matter knowledge, the repertoire of pedagogical skills the teachers possess to meet the needs of diverse learning situations, the degree of commitment to the profession, sensitivity to contemporary issues and problems as also to learners and the level of motivation critically influence the quality of curriculum transaction in the classrooms and thereby pupil learning and the larger processes of social learning.
>
> Teacher quality is a function of several factors: teachers' status, remuneration, conditions of work and their academic and professional education. The teacher education system through its initial and continuing professional development activities is expected to ensure an adequate supply of professionally competent teachers to run the nation's schools. Initial teacher education especially, has a major part to play in the making of a teacher. It marks the initiation of a novice entrant to the calling and as such has tremendous potential to imbue the would-be teacher with the aspirations, knowledge-base, repertoire of pedagogic capacities and humane attitudes.[1]

Apart from the fact that quality in teacher education is based on real life situations and involvements of all concerned with teacher ascent and excellence. It is time to regenerate a sense of all-embracing seriousness of purpose in redefining, re-analysing, re-executing and re-evaluating the finer essence of advancement in teacher education. The role of the society in penetrating deep into the philosophical aims and objectives in quest of quality in teacher education also demands a fresh and sustained approach as worthy and reliable stakeholders of education. Despite the fact that quality is nowhere given importance in reality in the teeth of numerous constraints consisting of financial and other liabilities for reshuffling and enriching knowledge-based and experience-happy teaching, motivation, interest, skill and other allied components accelerating quality and encouraging teachers to be iconoclastic and inspiring, quality in teacher education, let us frankly admit, wails in sheer passivity and misdirection, absence of profound vision and concern for excellence and the beyond. Where is the promise and perfection for quality march: 'To strive, to seek, to find, and not to yield'?

Indeed, the importance of quality enrichment by means of assuring and consolidating a very strong philosophical foundation can hardly be overemphasised. Fifteen years back what was categorically stressed by the Report to UNESCO of the International Commission on Education for the twenty-first century needs a rethinking:

> The importance of the quality of teaching, and therefore of teachers, cannot be overemphasised. It is at an early stage of basic education that the principal attitudes toward learning as well as the self-image of the learner are formed. The role of the teacher at this stage is crucial. The greater the handicaps the children coming to school have to overcome—in terms of poverty, difficult social environment or physical impairments—the greater demands on the teacher. He or she, to be effective, must draw upon a broad range of teaching skills, as well as on the human qualities of empathy, patience and humility, as a complement to authority. When a child's or adult's first teacher is poorly trained and poorly motivated, the very foundations on which all subsequent learning will be built will be unsound.

> The Commission feels that reasserting the importance of teachers in basic education and improving teachers' qualifications are tasks to which all governments must address themselves. The measures needed to recruit future teachers from among the most motivated students, improve their training and encourage the best among them to take on the most difficult posts need to be determined in relation to the specific circumstances of each country; but such measures must be taken, since, without them, it is unlikely that there will be significant improvements in quality where they are most needed.[2]

The fundamental philosophy that works prominently in the enrichment of quality in teacher education is a positive mental attitude that calls forth introspection backed and promised by further verified and well-reflected introspection in the diverse areas of quality sustenance and quality refinements. It should be noted that teaching teachers for the end-in-view of quality teaching necessitates endless and cautious experiments on removing the constraints of living efflorescence in teaching. Quality improvement is not a magical affair. Nor does it succeed in the absence of cultivation of finer sensibilities or values. Quality marches on in an assembly of good teamwork in quest of newer avenues and in negotiating any pitfall or incompetency that overpowers innovative, creative and reflective thinking and rightful action.

The involvement of a teacher learner or a teacher educator is a promise to be translated in the philosophy of aesthetics where quality enrichment heavily banks upon some of the essential components of exercise and evaluation of finer sensibilities like moderation, adherence to duties and responsibilities, appropriate and controlled methodology of teaching where every item of knowledge, understanding and information is fine-tuned and adorned with simplicity and serenity, proximity and cordiality in teaching-learning interactions. In this connection, one might recall Professor Highet's advice:

> Whatever you arc teaching, make it clear. Make it as firm as stone and as bright as sunlight. Not to yourself—that is easy. Make it clear to the people you are teaching—that is difficult.

> The difficulty lies partly in subject-matter, and partly language. You must think, not what you know, but what they do not know; not what you find hard, but what they will find hard; then, after putting yourself inside their minds, obstinate or puzzled, groping or mistaken as they are, explain what they need to learn. And you must be sure they understand your words. A strange name, a phrase only vaguely understood, will blur an explanation badly. Abstract words mean little on first hearing. Illustrate them. Give pictures and examples. And whenever possible, make sure you have been understood, by talking over what you have been trying to teach. A good pupil is seldom silent.[3]

In the name of digital advancement, teacher education, too, is undergoing constraints in quality acceleration from the subjective and individualistic points of view. An ever-increasing access to information by dwarfing freedom of imagination and action has brought the twenty-first century at the citadel of greater democracy sans individuality and the relation between quantitative and qualitative information and appreciation is fantastically stigmatised so much so that authoritarianism has become the only watchword in advancement or enrichment. That today's over-craziness and contingency in the trustworthiness in quality security, potency and variety are very much jeopardised is due to the fact that we, in the arena of teaching learning, do not have that freedom of exercising subjectivity under appalling economic and social ostracism or polarisation in communion with aggravating discontent:

> The digital revolution has contributed to the high degree of redundancy and job obsolescence in the manufacturing and increasing in the service sector, to the decline of middle management and the middle class, to mass and on-going unemployment and to the rise of a permanent underclass. The information revolution makes promises about social and cultural riches and opportunities. However, it can only keep these promises to a fortunate few. For many it spells disaster. And, for global and national societies as a whole, it points the way to dangerous economic and social polarisation and accelerating disenfranchisement of major sections of the population.[4]

Moreover, when quality is at crossroads with exercise of critical approach to the learner and the teacher in teacher education, the philosophy of teaching and learning is to be diluted in drab, dull, mechanical, authoritative and a superficial climate of regulation and regimentation. The positive role of the teacher or the learner is thus camouflaged in artificiality and the absence of freedom and joy which is the soul of true teaching-learning:

> Given that technological competence is a new basic in education, equal access and equal competence must be a basic concern for educators. Such competence will have an impact on students' quality of education and their access to jobs and retaining, to government information and to learning about critical issues which affect their lives. A consideration of the manner in which all basic needs can be met is crucial. However, as I have shown, it is commonly expected that as new technologies converse and the information super highway develops, they will have an ever-increasing impact on our work, leisure, health, life-style and national and cultural identities and social relationships. Nevertheless, little educational attention is being paid to the manner in which we produce and consume such technologies and to associated issues of politics and justice. We must encourage students to consider the social and cultural issues that are implicated in these possible transformations to the ways in which we 'live, work and play'. Be in the workplace, the home or elsewhere, students need to be in a position to assess the costs and benefits of the new communications media and to make-wise choices which maximise the economic, social and cultural benefits and minimise the risks and costs.[5]

Teacher education necessitates newer horizons of enrichment with cultivation of inwardness. Ascent and excellence are the pillars of enrichment. For enrichment and innovations in quality appreciation, teacher education should consider the following factors which are closely related to its in-depth vision: quality training, teaching materials, teacher educators, management and supervision. As regards quality training, the world of work should become creative and reflective, co-operative and judicious, scientific and value-vibrant. Teacher educators ought to upgrade the spirit of quality teaching in tune with application of curriculum renewals in upgrading skills and attitudes, aptitudes and appreciation. The fundamental point of attention for quality enrichment and excellence in teacher education should, therefore, be learning what and how to teach. As the Delors Commission significantly reminds us:

> The world in general is evolving so rapidly today that teachers, like most other professional groups, now must face the fact that their initial training will not see them through the rest of their lives: they need to update and improve their own knowledge and techniques throughout their lifetime. A careful balance has to be struck between competence in the subject taught and competence in teaching. In some countries, the system is criticised for neglecting method; in others, overemphasis on method, it is felt, produces teachers who know too little about their subject. Both are needed: neither should be sacrificed to the other in initial or in-service training. Teacher training has additionally to inculcate a view of teaching that transcends the utilitarian and encourages questioning, interaction and the consideration of several alternative hypotheses. One of the main functions of teacher education, both pre-service and in-service, is to equip teachers with the ethical, intellectual and emotional wherewithal to develop the same range of qualities in their pupils, as society demands.
>
> Good-quality training entails bringing trainee teachers into contact with experienced teachers as well as with researchers in their particular disciplines. Regular opportunities should be offered for practising teachers to learn through group-work sessions and through in-service courses. The reinforcement of in-service training, offered in as flexible a form as possible, can contribute a great deal to enhancing the skills and motivation of teachers, and improving their status. Given the importance of research into the qualitative improvement of teaching, teacher education should include a stronger component of training for research, and linkages between teacher training institutions and universities should be further strengthened.[6]

Quality enrichment in teacher education right now necessitates the end-in-view of the challenging teacher who ought to be radical and representative, conscious and careful. In fact, a certain sense of celebration of awareness in teacher education is still to be practised with all earnestness and sincerity of purpose. Let us frankly admit that we are still in the early age in preparing professional and humane teacher. The vision of teacher and teacher education needs a series of approaches to living and pulsating, intensive and penetrating as the National Curriculum Framework for Teacher Education reminds us:

> While the search for a philosophy of teacher education that satisfies the needs of our times continues, we seem to be converging on certain broad principles that should inform the enterprise. First, our thinking on teacher education is *integrative* and *eclectic*. It is free from the hold of 'schools' of philosophy and psychology. We also do not think of teacher education as a prescriptive endeavour; we want it to be open and flexible. Our emphasis is on changing contexts and our aim is to empower the teacher to relate himself/herself to them. Second, modern teacher education functions under a global canvas created by the concepts of 'learning society', 'learning to learn' and 'inclusive education'. The concern is to make teacher education *liberal, humanistic* and responsive to the demands *inclusive education*. The emphasis on teaching is not on didactic communication but on *non-didactic and dialogical explorations*. Third, modern pedagogy derives its inspiration more from *sociological and anthropological* insights on education. There is increasing recognition of the worth and potential of social context as a source for rejuvenating teaching and learning. *Multi-cultural education* and *teaching for diversity* are the needs of contemporary times. Fourth, we acknowledge the existence of a *diversity of learning spaces and curriculum sites* (firm, workplace, home. Community and media), apart from the classroom. We also appreciate the diversity of learning styles that children exhibit and learning contexts in which teachers have to function—over-sized class-rooms, language, ethnic and social diversities, children

> suffering disadvantages of different kinds. Lastly, we have realised the tentative and fluid nature of the so-called knowledge-base of teacher education. This makes *reflective practice* the central aim of teacher education. Pedagogical knowledge has to constantly undergo adaptation to meet the needs of diverse contexts through critical reflections by the teacher his/her practices. Teacher education needs to build capacities in the teachers to construct knowledge, to deal with different contexts and to develop the abilities to discern and judge in moments of uncertainty and fluidity, characteristic of teaching-learning environments.[7]

The vision of teacher and teacher education always welcomes finer sensibilities to be exercised by paying importance to individual process of development. We need to develop a different mind-set where oddities are rewards in the sense that they bring forth new challenges and new steps of advancement and enrichment. This is all the more important in preparing professional and humane teacher.

Quality assessment and accreditation for enrichment in teacher education should have a sound philosophical background. The benchmark of progress should be steered by a positive approach to the accreditation apposite and beyond. Quality never allows stagnancy nor does it allow negativism. It should always be accelerated in terms of excellence and ascent. Therefore, the enrichment of teacher education is a quality concern which is never-ending and always advancing. Unless this is taken into serious consideration, assessment and accreditation whatsoever can never be responsive to the call of the beyond as Professor Gautam has recently reminded us:

> The most important consideration is benchmarking the accreditation processes. Its credibility and acceptability is really the cornerstone of making the process and the outcome usable. It will be worthwhile reflecting why the innumerable awards conferred by India and Indians almost end up by being suspects and why awards received outside India receive so much acclaim. There are other questions: why is the publication, in a foreign journal so valued and a publication in an Indian

> journal does not get the same kind of recognition? There is a real possibility that nearly all Indians suspect each other's judgements, integrity. Perhaps, we, as a people, are a community which believes in contacts and leveraging for desired outcomes, possibly for more than other ethnic groups. The powerful rule the day and it works everywhere from crime and punishment to awards and recognition. How far this is true would need a scientific survey to understand and that is yet to come. However, the perception is fairly universal and common to salvage the process of accreditation from this pervasive feeling will be the first task which professionals would need to address. This cannot be done by a Regulatory Authority or even political leadership. This has to be done by the people who are affected and who operate the system. It is going to be an uphill task. We live in an era where convenience of decision-making in administration is often applauded and firmness and straight forward talk very often is resented and often debunked. A lax administrator is credited with the epithet of a 'King' and a strict one is abused. Caste men, people from the same religion, people from shared backgrounds and persons from common educational institutions, all expect favoured treatment from the key decision makers. Bounties are meant to be exchanged. In such an environment, lending credibility to accreditation process is going to be a demanding task. We need to think about these things carefully, slowly widening the circle of awareness. In conducting ourselves the way we very often do, does not serve the objectives of accreditation and could well cost us international credibility. The time to raise these questions is now. The time to reflect and work towards a resolution of this complex situation in the right direction is now.[8]

Admittedly, we will have to go many more miles for enrichment and beyond in teacher education. No doubt, there are challenges more difficult and more painstaking, more intricate and more disturbing but who denies that quality enrichment is a matter that always demands right thoughts, right principles, right procedures and right strategies of action?

Are we, in the profession of teaching, joining hands together in our adventure for excellence and ascent?

References

1. *National Curriculum Framework for Teacher Education,* National Council for Teacher Education, New Delhi, 2009, pp. 1-2.
2. *Learning: The Treasure Within,* Report to UNESCO of the International Commission on Education for the Twenty-first Century, UNESCO Publishing, 1996, pp. 146-147.
3. Highet, Gilbert: *The Art of Teaching, Methuen,* University Paperbacks, London, 1963, p. 246.
4. Paechter, Carrie *et. al.*: *Knowledge, Power and Learning,* Paul Chapman Publishing Limited, London in association with the Open University UK, 2001, p. 163.
5. *Ibid.,* p. 165.
6. *Learning: The Treasure Within,* Report to UNESCO of the International Commission on Education for the Twenty-first Century, UNESCO Publishing, 1996, pp. 149-150.
7. *National Curriculum Framework for Teacher Education,* National Council for Teacher Education, New Delhi, 2009, pp. 19-20.
8. Gautam, Vinayshil, "For Accreditation and Beyond", *NAAC News,* National Assessment and Accreditation Council, Bangalore, January 2012, p. 3.

2 Post-accreditation Strategies for Quality Sustenance in Teacher Education: Aesthetic Parameters

Teaching is a complex and challenging activity. Teaching teachers is a more complex and challenging activity because it calls forth assurance of quality sustenance and excellence from diverse points of view. Mere quality sustenance is never an endpoint but a beginning one. This also necessitates assurance of the manifold and interesting, diverse and divergent parameters which not only consolidate but also enrich quality that knows no end. As quality sustenance in teacher education is an exciting and alluring process of advancement, every effort in undertaking any strategy should be strengthened with the spirit of aesthetic enquiry in particular.

The accreditation of an educational institution is simply an initial passport to quality-quest and sustenance-shield. This does not at all mean an end to our march for quality. Rather is it a fillip to advancement in a more judicious, logical, positive, thrilling and challenging involvement where both the academic and the administrative activities of an institution of teacher education in particular are solemnly harmonised for consolidation and an onward quest for greater and finer exposures of quality and excellence. As a matter of fact, teacher education takes an altogether stimulating avenue of aesthetic fine-tuning when the different strategic procedures are remodelled in the nuances of aesthetic sensibilities. These also eliminate dullness and drabness in our day-to-day academic assignments.

In any institutional accreditation to the maintenance and furtherance of quality and excellence, a few strategic areas are identified, analysed and evaluated in terms of a few specific components related thereto so much so that identification of quality exercise never remains absent in any form. Despite this fact, there might be some occasions where the essential purpose of accreditation for dynamism in enrichment gets a severe jolt on account of the fact that everything is looked upon as a mechanical process where freedom of involvement and joy of teaching-learning get lost in the strategic vision and exercise for the follow-up programmes in re-accreditation. As a matter of fact, it has more often than not been found that an institution already accredited does not take any interest in re-accreditation because confusion is worse confounded in the mapping and execution of re-accreditation programmes in communicated and conjoint strategies of academic and administrative activities in tune with aesthetic simplicity and serenity of enrichment.

Curriculum plays a vital role in any educational institution especially teacher education institution. It is a harmonious combination of the subject(s) to be taught and activities to be considered and executed in such a way that both theoretical and practical activities are fine-tuned in the spirit of aesthetics. It means that mere curriculum design and development with some specific ends-in-view may invite discipline and regularity but that may not ensure interest and attitude orientation nor does it ensure aptitude and appreciation firmly-based on aesthetic design and development. This also affects academic flexibility on the part of a teacher-educator who fails to ignite and kindle the spirit of aesthetic appreciation. Curriculum design and development, as such, cannot be a pointer to the enrichment of knowledge, understanding, skills and appreciation output unless there is a firm assurance that the learner enjoys aesthetic criticism in dealing with some facts or components where learning comes a cropper.

Continual curriculum feedback through aesthetic design and development for that purpose welcomes five factors especially related to the subjective patterns of teaching-learning. These are:

(a) The teacher-educator's own process of thinking in aesthetics where the particular components like goodness, truth and beauty are delineated in terms of subjectivity.

(b) The syntax and stylistics of aesthetics are crystallised with special reference to the items of teaching-learning.

(c) The mapping and analysis of all aesthetic strategies as the teacher-educator deems apposite and appropriate ought to be revised and reoriented with special reference to learner-attitude and learner-appreciation. It might occasionally demand that the learner enjoys full freedom and responsibility where the strategies are his or her own, very own.

(d) The strategies for refinement in teaching-learning should be regularly and reasonably analysed and evaluated in order to make it as foolproof and purposeful as possible.

(e) Any strategy for the enrichment calls forth aesthetic fullness of appreciation the ultimate outcome of which should always ensure the joy of teaching and learning. In fact, a strategy becomes meaningful and worthwhile only when it is ensured that there is a perennial interest of enrichment and advancement, excellence and further excellence.

Admittedly, curriculum feedback is a never-ending strategy for advancement in education. But that does not necessarily mean a device or a strategy that suffers from passivity and mechanical approach. It may sometimes so happen that one forsakes feedback on curriculum in order to ensure joy and freedom. If joy and freedom, the vital components in the exercise of aesthetic sensibilities are lost in the melee of the parasitical strategy which is rest assured with feedback purpose and fails to become a part and parcel of advancement endeavour, education becomes absolutely meaningless and stalls like a silent colossus.

Teaching, learning and evaluation very much suffer from self-satisfaction. This is particularly remarkable in the case of educational institutions which have already been accredited and, obviously, await re-accreditation. What actually happens is that in the name of teaching, learning and evaluation practically nothing is pre-ensured which means with the enjoyment of initial accreditation it becomes unhindrance to further advancement and excellence. As already stated, neither education nor teaching-learning enjoys eternal holidays and can never be a limited affair. This is further approved by the fact that any accreditation whatsoever or howsoever to an educational institution is never a pointer to an end-point of learning, teaching and quality. Whatever quality is accredited should be sustained and enriched and this should be a never-ending process. Actually, quality maintenance and quality boost demand an aesthetic approach where both the teacher and the learner become very sincere to any strategy undertaken in the post-accreditation period. This is why curriculum feedback in sync with academic flexibility becomes very much aware of teaching, learning and evaluation. The significant points of aesthetics are dealt with the process of teaching-learning which starts from the admission process and the student-teacher profile of the institution. It does not require any specific explanation that there is no coordination between the admission process and the student profile. At the same time, it is undeniable that the role of the teacher is subject to debate in the very strategic processes of admission and preparation of the student profile. This also points to the fact that the aesthetics of catering to the diverse needs of both the teachers and the learners in an institution of teacher education is awfully neglected. When a teacher fails to become a learner-teacher, the strategies of teaching-learning cannot avert ukase. Secondly, the strategies of evaluation and reform consequential to teaching-learning also demand an aesthetic approach where all learners are to be directed towards the vision of quality learning and excellence. Evaluation for the sake of evaluation alone and reforms in the same pattern suffer from routine work. It is time right now or never to save our educational institutions, especially the institutions for teacher education, suffering from paranoia.

Teacher quality from the post-accreditational point of view in teacher education for promotion of aesthetic awareness looks forward to three essential components: one, teacher preparation and teacher involvement, two, the field of work with the healthy ambience of teaching-learning in tune with aesthetic involvement, and three, sustenance of excellence and quality to an extent of diversified programmes of action.

Research, consultancy and extension programmes in teacher education always look forward to aesthetic refinement. The components which come under the purview of the above are: promotion of research, research and publication output, consultancy and extension activities. What is essential is to thoroughly ponder over and implement each component which guarantees aesthetic awareness all the time and the teacher educator makes a holistic approach to every item of advancement. It is not a matter of time-bound experiment in every item of activity. Sometimes flexibility is required. This flexibility means a warm welcome to aesthetic thinking where pause, rhythm, accent, intonation or acceleration, as the case may be, would ensure newer directions of creative and critical thinking. A collaborative procedure with other educational organisations would be very effective provided that the mutually agreed formula of aesthetic endeavour allows further flexibility and newer avenues of teaching-learning for humane and professional advancement.

Admittedly, whatever effort is directed towards quality sustenance in teacher education initially requires an assembly of four essential components to be continually crystallised through aesthetic vision. These are: physical facilities for teaching-learning, appropriate maintenance of necessary infrastructure, easy availability of library as a perennial learning resource and the role of Information and Communication Technology (ICT). Indeed, today's concern for ICT in quest of quality advancement is to adequately and significantly introduce the philosophy of aesthetics in it. As a matter of fact, no information or communication becomes really very effective unless it is attuned to aesthetic thinking and experiment where the learner and the teacher are blessed with the joy of learning and teaching.

Quality maintenance and furtherance in teacher education become meaningless in the absence of pupil support and progression. It is therefore necessary to create a healthy atmosphere where pupils are voluntarily involved in activities and their involvements are continually supported from the standpoint of excellence and beyond. This is why teacher education should be very careful about all-embracing governance and leadership. The institutional vision and leadership should have a firm basis of aesthetics. This leads to sensitising organisational arrangements, strategy development and deployment, human resource management and management of finance and resources. These different components of governance and leadership in teacher education are very delicate, and therefore, calls forth a humane touch of aesthetic endeavour so that truth, as it were, engages in all efflorescence of fullness.

Innovations in teacher education are the life blood for sustenance of quality and advancement of excellence. If this life blood is to be recycled it requires constant monitoring of aesthetic values like righteousness and stick-to-it-iveness to transparency and transcendence, simplicity and natural efflorescence of in-depth vision for quality refinement. All innovative decisions should begin from the accreditation valuation already made and the suggestions put forward for further quality acceleration specially designed to arrest teaching-learning aesthetic stylistics. In fact, the rubrics of teaching-learning always prompt for redisigning strategies for advancing in quality with remarkable distinction of aesthetic serenity.

The curriculum framework plays a vital role in teacher education for quality sustenance. The organisation of aesthetic values needs special attention and, for this end-in-view, clubbing intellectual with aesthetic values plays a very characteristic role in quality sustenance and excellence. In this connection, the suggestions referred to by Professor Tyler in the report of the Social Studies Curriculum Committee of the Dalton Schools in New York City on values in terms of attitudes, intellect and aesthetics infusion are very useful and significant:

1. **Attitudes toward self**
   - 1.1. Growing from self-love to self-respect; acceptance of self-realisation of one's own worth.
   - 1.2. Integrity, honesty and frankness with self; objectively critical of self.
   - 1.3. Hopefulness for the future.
   - 1.4. Willingness for adventure; sense of mission, of reformation, of great crusade.
   - 1.5. Desire to make a productive contribution, not to be a parasite.
2. **Attitudes towards others**
   - 2.1. Respect for the dignity and worth of every human being, regardless of his racial, national, economic or social status.
   - 2.2. Cherishing variety in people, opinions, acts.
   - 2.3. Equality of opportunity for all.
   - 2.4. Tolerance, goodwill, kindliness.
   - 2.5. Desire for justice for all.

3. **Attitudes toward social groups to which he belongs**
   3.1. Loyalty to world society and world order.
   3.2. Acceptance of social responsibility.
   3.3. Willingness to submit one's problems to group study and group judgement.
   3.4. Balance of integrity of individual and group participation.
   3.5. Loyalty to social purposes of the group rather than undiscriminating loyalty to whatever the group does.
   3.6. Willingness to work for an abundance of the good things of life for all peoples in the world.
4. **Intellectual and aesthetic values**
   4.1. Love of truth, however disconcerting it may be.
   4.2. Respect for work well done, worth of socially direct effort as well as achievement.
   4.3. Freedom of thought, expression and worship.
   4.4. Love of beauty in art, in surroundings, in the lives of people.
   4.5. Respect for reasonable procedures rather than force as the only proper and workable way of getting along together.[1]

The strategies for quality sustenance in teacher education at the post-accreditation stage in line with aesthetic thinking and programmed activities need continuous, careful and fool-proof promises of perfection and poignancy. In this connection, the role, philosophy, purpose and practice of teacher education necessitate an aesthetic approach to be justified in preparing and translating the vision of education for fullness in humane sensitisation from the following points of view suggested by the National Council for Teacher Education:

- Teachers need to be prepared to care for children, enjoy to be with them, seek knowledge, own responsibility towards society and work to build a better world, develop sensitivity to the problems of the learners, commitment to justice and zeal for social reconstruction.
- Teachers need to view learners as active participants in their own learning and not as mere recipients of knowledge; need to

encourage their capacity to construct knowledge; ensure that learning shifts away from rote methods. Learning is to be viewed as a search for meaning out of personal experiences and knowledge generation as a continuously evolving process of reflective learning.

- Teacher education must engage with theory along with field experiences to help trainees to view knowledge not as external to the learner but as something that is actively constructed during learning. Teacher education should integrate academic knowledge and professional learning into a meaningful whole.
- Teachers need to be trained in organising learner-centred, activity-based participatory learning experiences-play, projects, discussion, dialogue, observation, visits, integrating academic learning with productive work.
- Teacher education should engage teachers with the curriculum, syllabi and textbooks to critically examine them rather than taking them as 'given' and accepted without question. Teacher education should provide opportunity to student-teachers for reflection and independent study without packing the training schedule with teacher-directed activities alone.
- The programme should engage teachers with children in real contexts rather than teach them about children through theories alone. It should help them understand the psycho-social attributes and needs of learners, their special abilities and characteristics, their preferred mode of cognition, motivation and learning resulting from home and community socialisation.
- The programme should help teachers or potential teachers to develop social sensitivity and consciousness and finer human sensibilities.
- Teacher education programmes need to broaden the curriculum (both school and teacher education) to include different traditions of knowledge; educate teachers to connect school knowledge with community knowledge and life outside the school.
- Teacher education programmes need to help teachers appreciate the potentials of hands-on experience as a pedagogic medium

both inside and outside the classroom; and work as integral to the process of education.

- Teachers need to re-conceptualise citizenship education in terms of human rights and approaches of critical pedagogy; emphasise environment and its protection, living in harmony within oneself and with natural and social environment; promote peace, democratic way of life, constitutional values of equality, justice, liberty, fraternity and secularism, and caring values.
- In view of the many-sided objectives of teacher education the evaluation protocol needs to be comprehensive and provide place for the evaluation of attitudes, values, dispositions, habits and hobbies, in addition to the conceptual and pedagogical aspects through appropriate quantitative as well as qualitative parameters.[2]

For a renewal, regeneration and sustenance of teacher education in quest of enrichment of quality and strengthening the vision of re-accreditation we will have to go many more miles so that the whole process of preparation for re-accreditation or post-accreditation undergoes an aesthetically bold and transparent, all-encapsulating and holistic approach in diverse strategies of refinement. It may be started from a revolutionary approach to redefining education and teaching in terms of the aesthetics of revolution as well as evolution in doing away with bookish education of reception-memorisation-repetition syndrome.

The socio-aesthetics of post-accreditation strategies for quality acceleration in teacher education is also to be forewarned with the dismal relationship between education and ownership of knowledge. One might recall the invaluable words of Young:

> Social definitions of educational value, [which] thus become problematic in the sense that if they persist it is not because knowledge is in any meaningful way best made available according to the criteria they represent, but because they are conscious or unconscious cultural choices which accord with the values and beliefs of dominant groups in a particular time.[3]

As the new definition of teacher educator welcomes the attribute "the serene path finder of meaningful teaching-learning", post-accreditation pre-supposes more meaningful reflective and inclusive teaching-learning. It is time now to rethink and re-establish meaningful learning —"a process in which new information is related to an existing relevant aspect of an individual's knowledge structure".[4]

The aggravating challenge in teacher education is to explore newer avenues of recognising and crystallising pupil ownership of knowledge and minimising the barrier between institutional knowledge and owned knowledge of learners. For meaningful learning the teacher should always bear in mind that,

> Meaningful learning occurs when new information is linked to existing concepts. Consequently, the most important single factor in learning is what the individual knows; the aim of the teacher should be to relate new material to this. In itself this is unproblematic. Confusion arises, however, when it is assumed that 'starting from where the learner is' necessarily means starting in the non-school context, and that, in doing this, the teacher will automatically bridge the divide between school and non-school knowledge. The argument seems to go like this; students will bring their own purposes and values to practical activity which may well precede and introduce them to high-status knowledge (such as school physics). Via a direct experience of activities made meaningful through their relationship to their real concerns, students will be better able to learn such higher-status knowledge.[5]

A major paradigm-shift from teaching to learning-teaching and comradeship with learners as the aesthetics of teaching warmly welcomes is one of the most serene avenues of progress in post-accreditation strategies. Moreover, as strategies, whatsoever and howsoever useful and dependable, should be analysed and evaluated for setting new benchmarks of advancement in teacher education in excellence and beyond that from time to time.

Are we prepared for launching our programmes of activities towards that direction in teacher education?

Meanwhile, let us muse within ourselves in the ever stimulating words of Tagore:

> "I thought that my voyage had come to its end at the last limit of my power, that the path before me was closed, that provisions were exhausted and the time come to take shelter in a silent obscurity".
>
> "But I find that thy will knows no end in me. And when old words die out on the tongue, new melodies break forth from the heart; and where the old tracks are lost, new country is revealed with its wonders".[6]

References

1. Tyler, Ralph W. : *Basic Principles of Curriculum and Instruction,* The University of Chicago Press, Chicago, 1949, pp. 92-93.
2. "Vision of Teacher Education", *National Curriculum Framework for Teacher Education,* National Council for Teacher Education, New Delhi, 2009, pp. 20-21.
3. Young, M.F.D. (Ed.): *"An Approach to the Study of Curricula as Socially Organised Knowledge",* Knowledge and Control, Macmillan, 1971, p. 38.
4. Novak, J.D.: *A Theory of Education,* Cornell University Press, Ithaca, 1977, p. 74.
5. Paechter, Carrie: "Schooling and the Ownership of Knowledge", in Carrie Paechter, Margaret Preedy, David Scott and Janet Soler (Ed.), *Knowledge, Power and Learning,* Paul Chapman Publishing Limited, London, 2001, p. 177.
6. Tagore, Rabindranath: *Gitanjali,* Macmillan India Limited, New Delhi, Macmillan Pocket Tagore Edition 1983, p. 21.

3 Teaching in the Twenty-first Century: Gandhian Perspectives

Teaching is a challenging activity. Teaching in the twenty-first century in tune with the philosophy of education for preparing our teachers as dynamic and responsible for enrichment and advancement as Mahatma Gandhi advocated is a more challenging one because it is under terrible constraints at present.

First, most of the teachers, let us frankly admit, are not aware of the Gandhian vision and mission of a teacher. Second, Gandhi's incomparable and unparalleled experiments and real-life approach to teaching have been unfortunately relegated to the so-called absence of practicability. Third, the mind-set of most of the teachers of today are alien to the inherent force of the Gandhian education of aesthetics which is more or less turned into a myth cradling confusion and utter ukase in understanding and appreciation. Fourth, a certain sense of the absence of exercise of finer sensibilities offering ample avenues of excellence in teaching has been sufficiently and inanely consumed by computer-crazy teaching where quality and excellence are curiously blended in terms of quantity and over-simplification well-awarded with an inward world of forced or devised barrenness. What a prize for education and the teacher as well! Amidst this catastrophe, the Gandhian philosophy of teaching is perhaps nowhere nurtured either in theory or in practice for the genuine efflorescence of inward vision in every human being.

Looking intensively into some of the fundamental characteristics of Mahatma Gandhi's philosophy of teaching which best incorporates the study of the body, mind and soul harmoniously blended and translated into action for fullness in all aspects of human life, the following components need revitalisation:

(i) The teacher ought to be a learner in learning each pupil's plus and the non-plus points of pursuit of knowledge. If he/she becomes very conscious on this point of pupil-activities and takes apposite and correct action, half the battle for imparting quality education is won.

(ii) The teacher ought to have an assured and vibrant mind-set. He/she is not only a teacher but a sincere task-master also who christens his/her pupils with self-dependence, self-activity, self-belief and self-enrichment. For all these, he/she actually serves as a role model to the pupils.

(iii) As a teacher's success in teaching entirely depends on the extinction of personality, he/she ought to reduce himself/herself into a cipher. No doubt, it is very difficult to be justified to this mandatory and ardent proposition, but no alternative to this practically suits the teaching profession that cares for quality and excellence.

(iv) Tolerance is the key to success in teaching. If the teacher judiciously accelerates this component and encourages the learners in exercising the same in their devotion and dedication to education, the teaching-learning climate either in the classroom or elsewhere undergoes a radical and revolutionary transformation.

(v) In the profession of teaching, the teacher ought to be humanistic and altruistic. The message of true teaching must guarantee cultivation of humane sensibilities and elimination of narrowness of vision in life and work.

The teachings of *sarir-sram, brahmacharya* and austerity as Gandhi advocates should be prioritised in education. These would enable the learners to learn a lot in their physical, moral and intellectual endeavour as enviable dividends. Today when our learners hardly take note of the importance of these essential components due to their adherence to an astonishingly appalling interest in gadgets of various types, thanks a lot to electronics and mass-media bringing about the mass moratorium in teaching-learning, it is time to reshuffle teaching for learning to be and learning for unhindered spontaneity.

Gandhi's concern for right teaching and right education of the learner and the society in a right climate that shows advancement and illumination calls forth a re-thinking of the ends-in-view of education in general and teacher education in particular. A teacher in the twenty-first century sincerely and truly responding to the Gandhian philosophy of education cannot but be reflective, creative, critical, probing, innovative and analytical in thought and action. He/she takes recourse to cohesive control and discipline in letter and spirit to arrive at a point of poignancy in vision and action. This is not an easy task. It necessitates endless self-training where the seedlings of success are nurtured with ample care and caution. What Gandhi thinks about values in teaching is a celebration of awareness in the arena of teaching and learning in a conjoint, harmonious and communicated altar of purity and serenity of truth, goodness and beauty.

If the entire world is to respond and vibrate in the classroom, the teacher as Gandhi envisions and experiments through *Nai Talim,* ought to be intellectually alert and practically instrumental to the creation and re-creation of an ideal ambience of what the twenty-first century strives for 'learning to be' in association with 'learning to live together' for fullness in education. Let our new education for better teaching welcome the essence of Gandhian strategies for teaching in tune with the positive suggestions delivered by dedicated and devoted teachers of excellence. Let the education of bread-labour through the education of the spinning wheel be translated by means of a remodelled framework of the curriculum where teachers are active practitioners of enlightened education promising further advancement of the learners in auto-education.

The primary role of the teacher is to enable his/her learner to identify and expand the sky of the mind - *cidakas*—unexplored and underestimated in inane ends-in-view of education. The intensive lesson of the spinning wheel as Gandhi has introduced has the priceless essence of detachment from extravagance and affluence, greed and pride, anger and unhappiness, to mention a few of the dreadful ills of matter-of-fact, stereotyped, mechanical and commonality-crushed teaching-learning. If today's teacher fails to stimulate our learners to become *amritasya putrah,* the ever victorious death-defying emblems of spirituality in the resonance of action of the *charkha*—the spinning wheel—the world of education and, for that end-in-view, teaching will continually bemoan in the Shakespearean ecstasy: "Mischief, thou art afoot"!

As regards the role of the teacher in teaching the Gandhian philosophy of non-violence, the less said the better. Who ignores that education in the twenty-first century miserably discards the importance of sincere adherence to *Satyagraha* which propagates absolute acceptance of and respect for Truth and stands for 'the still small voice within' everyone? One might recall Gandhi's invaluable words: "The still small voice within you must always be the final arbiter when there is a conflict of duty."[1]

The teacher in the twenty-first century ought to reorient strategies of teaching for translating the Gandhian philosophy of Truth and non-violence, and teach so as to baptise love-lost learners to accentuate love-force, truth-force or soul-force in the pursuit of meaningful, living, purposeful and humane education. "Sacrifice everything", as Gandhi prompts us, "except truth and non-violence."[2]

Unless a radical paradigm-shift in the role of the teacher in the Gandhian dimensions of teaching to explore delight and freedom is happily wedded to the ten-fold path of *Sarvodaya* or Universal Dawn, crisis in education will continually aggravate: *Abhaya, Ahimsa, Nyaya, Brahmacharya, Sparsabhavana, Sarvadharma-samabhavana, Swadeshi, Sarir-srama, Pararthabhavana* and *Satyagraha* are not only significant as eternal values for a changing society but also the characteristic components of transparency and transcendence in teaching-learning. The twenty-first century looks forward to beginning a new and thrilling programme of teaching where the Gandhian philosophy of *Satyagraha* acts as a hallmark in teaching how to love the so-called enemies who have unfortunately been denied the warmth of togetherness of man despite numerous differences. As Gandhi observes on the teacher's role in imparting lessons on Truth as Love that wins over all constraints:

> Love those that despitefully use you. It is easy for you to love your friends. But I say unto you, love your enemies.[3]

Gandhi wants the teacher to provide his/her learners with ample opportunities for unfolding the inner spirit of *Satyagraha*. He characteristically asserts:

> It is never the intention of a *Satyagrahi* to embarrass a wrong-doer. The appeal is never to his fear. It is, must be, always to his heart. The *Satyagrahi's* object is to convert, not to coerce, the wrong-doer. He should avoid artificiality in all his doings. He acts naturally and from inward conviction.[4]

whether Whither teaching now? Where is the teaching that responds to the education of the heart by challenging all constraints against effulgence of Truth?

Socialism as we come across in the day-to-day life immersed in workaholic madness spreading its canvas in teaching-learning is a premonition to annihilation of humanism. Gandhi's prescription for realising and accentuating socialistic humanism invites the attention of the teacher to three important perspectives. One, true socialism stands for the emancipation of man who combines reality with socialism. It is neither weaving in the air nor capitalising cheap popularity in the name of closeness to the society. It is life-centric, value-centric and reason-centric. It cares for turning each narrow "I" to the all-embracing "We". To impart any lesson on socialism in a heterogeneous classroom atmosphere through conjoint and communicated learning to love and live together is to march for education of ascent and excellence. Two, to embrace true socialism is to broaden the world of humanity with love, compassion and kindred aura of sympathy. Gandhi considers the teaching of humane altruism a must in order to avert social ostracism, an ailment from which education now suffers almost everywhere. Three, the Gandhian philosophy of education is perhaps the only antidote to apathy and ignorance nursed in utter passivity writ large in man and society.

Gandhi's altruistic vision of education for cultivation of human rights demands a re-thinking and re-translating in renewed practice in teaching-learning. It should be the role of the teacher to involve the learners in the

Gandhian philosophy of human rights in theory and practice under a new curriculum framework where idealising and practising human rights become natural and spontaneous, vibrant and effective. As a guideline for the human rights activist, every teacher recalls the invaluable words of Gandhi:

> He must be completely free from anger and lust, greed and attachment, pride and fear. He must reduce himself to zero and have perfect control over all his senses—beginning with the palate or tongue. Tongue is the organ of speech as well as of taste. It is with the tongue that we indulge in exaggeration, untruth and speech that hurts. The craving for taste makes us slaves to the palate so that like animals we live to eat. But with proper discipline, we can make ourselves into being only 'a little below the angels'. He who has mastered his senses is first and foremost among men. All virtues reside in him. God manifests Himself through him. Such is the power of self-discipline.[5]

Simultaneously, Gandhi asserts for education that prompts one to devote to the learning of self-realisation, and, for that end-in-view, teacher education should be directed towards the training of student-teachers and freshers to undergo practice of how to inspire the learners in the classroom to prove their worth in self-realisation. As a positive pointer to this, he humbly submits:

> What I want to achieve—what I have been striving and pinning to achieve these thirty years—is self-realisation, to see God face to face, to attain *Moksha.* I live and move and have my being in pursuit of this goal. All that I do by way of speaking and writing, and all my ventures in the political field, are directed to this same end. I am but a weak aspirant, ever failing, ever trying. My failures make me more vigilant than before and intensify my faith. I can see with the eye of faith that the observance of the twin doctrines of Truth and Non-violence has possibilities of which we have but very inadequate conception.[6]

Teacher education needs to be overhauled by taking into serious consideration the quest for Truth not only in theory but also in practice. The aroma of Truth is the most energising and significant factor in the teaching of self-discipline as a prominent symbol of self-excellence. Gandhian emphasises on the study of Truth as the vehicle of appreciating one's inwardness of vision which is spirituality:

> What is true of God is true, though in a less degree, of the assumption of the truth of the fundamental moralities. As a matter of fact, they are implied in the belief in God or Truth. Departure from these has landed the truants in endless misery. Difficulty in practice should not be confused with disbelief. A Himalayan expedition has also its prescribed conditions of success. Difficulty of fulfilling the conditions does not make the expedition impossible. It only adds more interest and jest to the search. Well, this expedition in search of God or Truth is infinitely more than numberless Himalayan expeditions and, therefore, much more interesting. If we have no jest for it, it is because of the weakness of our faith. What we see with our physical eyes is more real to us than the only reality. We know that the appearances are deceptive. And yet we treat trivialities and realities. To see the trivialities as such is half the battle won. It constitutes more than half the search after Truth or God.
>
> Unless we disengage ourselves from these trivialities, we have not even the leisure for the great search, or is it to be reserved for our leisure hours?[7]

When would teaching for self-discipline be introduced?

Teacher education as Gandhi strongly believes must bring about a very sensitive and positive change for the teaching of socio-aesthetics. Student-teachers and others associated with this very significant assignment should evolve and experiment with newer parameters of teaching the learners how to be social by exercising aesthetic sensibilities. For this purpose, he introduces the spinning wheel as the most ideal means of learning through joyful activities in an atmosphere of freedom, self-dependence and self-awareness to what stands for and accelerates the spirit of Truth, Goodness and Beauty for everyone in the society. That the message of the teaching as such with the spinning is altruism gets a new dimension in the introduction of the spinning wheel for self-learning. What Gandhi has observed in 1931 on the role of the spinning wheel for the development of aesthetic and social regeneration as follows is equally applicable at present and should form one of the benchmarks of advancement in teacher education for socio-aesthetic consciousness:

> The *Charkha* is a useful and indispensable article for every home. It is the symbol of the nation's prosperity and therefore freedom. It is a symbol not of commercial war but of commercial peace. It bears not a message of ill-will towards the nation's of the earth but of goodwill and self-help. It will not need a navy threatening the world's peace and exploiting its resources; but it needs the religious determination of millions to spin their yarn in their own homes as today they cook their food in their own homes.[8]

The spirit of socio-aesthetic consciousness that the teacher educator wants her/his learners under the diverse programmes of training through demonstration of lessons in the practice of the spinning wheel as Gandhi has introduced in Basic Education needs a look afresh:

> My plan to impart primary education through the medium of village handicrafts like spinning and carding, etc., is thus conceived as a silent social revolution fraught with the most far-reaching consequences. It will provide a healthy and moral basis of relationship between the city and the village and thus go a long way towards eradicating some of the worst evils of the present social insecurity and poisoned relationship between the classes. It will check the progressive decay of our villages and lay the foundation of a just social order in which there is no unnatural division between the 'haves' and the 'have-nots' and everybody is assured of a living wage and the right to freedom. And all this would be accomplished without the horror of a bloody class war or a colossal capital expenditure such as would be involved in the mechanisation of a vast continent like

> India. Nor would it entail a helpless dependence on foreign imported machinery or technical skill. Lastly, by obviating the necessity for highly specialised talent, it would place the destiny of the masses, as it were, in their own hands.[9]

The spirit of *Sarvodaya* or Universal Dawn that Gandhi has recommended for cultivation of socio-aesthetic consciousness should also come under the purview of education in general and teacher education in particular. As this component forms an inseparable part of humanistic and living education, the framework of teacher education should welcome a wider platform for training of teachers in the guidance and supervision of every learner's excellence in the manifestation of behaviour. How the learners learn how to think and act almost entirely depends on how pure and perfect they are in the exercise of their thoughts, words and deeds. Gandhi's concern for all these is how the learners are trained in *Brahmacharya* which is nothing but the knowledge and exercise of self-control, self-purity and self-perfection, the role of the teacher is not to teach directly through some stereotyped lessons as course of studies but inspire every learner to learn by her/his own way of learning through impetus received from teachers or others in the most distinctive ways in perfection. Gandhi elucidates:

> *Brahmacharya* must be observed in thought, word and deed. It may be harmful to suppress the body, if the mind is at the same time allowed to go astray. Where the mind wanders, the body must follow sooner or later.
>
> It is necessary here to appreciate a distinction. It is one thing to allow the mind to harbour impure thoughts; it is a different thing altogether if it strays among them in spite of ourselves. Victory will be ours in the end, if we non-cooperate with the mind in its evil wanderings.
>
> We experience every moment of our lives, that often while the body is subject to our control, the mind is not. This physical control should never be relaxed, and in addition we must put forth a constant endeavour to bring the mind under control.[10]

Even in the teaching of religion, Gandhi maintains the same socio-aesthetic spirit of *Sarvodaya.* Here the concept of *Sarvadharma-Samabhavava* or the idea of conceptualising all religions as one and the same acts the fundamental principle of teaching. It also allows the teacher to enable the learners to broaden their visions on religion and widen their sensibilities to be shared on an altruistic basis. Gandhi characteristically observes:

> After long study and experience, I have come to the conclusion that (1) all religions are true; (2) all religions have some error in them; (3) all religions are almost as dear to me as my own man beings should be as dear to one's own close relatives. My own veneration for other faiths is the same as that for my own faith; therefore, no thought of conversion is possible. The aim of the Fellowship should be to help a Hindu become a better Hindu, a Mussalman to become a better Mussalman, and a Christian a better Christian. The attitude of patronising toleration is false to the spirit of International Fellowship. If I have a suspicion in my mind that my own religion is more or less true, and that others' are more or less false, instead of being more or less true, then, though I may have some sort of fellowship with them, it is of an entirely different kind from the one we need in the International Fellowship. Our prayer for the other must be NOT 'God, give him the light that Thou has given me' BUT 'Give him all the light and truth he needs for his highest development'. Pray merely that your friends may become men, whatever their form of religion.[11]

Bearing in mind, the education of toleration it is also important to inspire learners how to nurture curiosity with utmost care and attention. The training of teachers teaching children at the elementary stage should, as Gandhi emphasises, include how to accelerate and qualify every component of teaching towards better attention and motivation to the curiosity of every child. If the teacher involves the child in the proper cultivation of curiosity, teaching becomes meaningful and justified. Gandhi's observation on this point is very significant at present:

> As regards children's curiosity about the fact of life, we should tell them if we know, and admit our ignorance if we do not. If it is something that must not be told, we should check them and ask them not to put such questions even to anyone else. We must never put them off. They know more things than we imagine. If they do not know and if we refuse to tell them, they try to acquire knowledge in a questionable manner. But if it has to be withheld from them, we must take such risk.[12]

It is interesting to note in this connection that Gandhi's educational philosophy of non-violence is directed towards elimination of fear and emancipation of the spirit of the *Atman*. This enables the learner how to safeguard self-dignity and self-liberation. Gandhi's own interpretation in this respect is noteworthy:

> Just as one must learn the art of killing in the training for violence, so one must learn the art of dying in the training for non-violence. Violence does not mean emancipation from fear, but discovering the means of combating the cause of fear. Non-violence, on the other hand, has no cause for fear. The votary of non-violence has to cultivate the capacity for sacrifice of the highest type in order to be free from fear. He wrecks not if he should lose his land, his wealth, his life. He who has not overcome all fear cannot practise *ahimsa* to perfection. The votary of *ahimsa* has only one fear, that is of God. He who seeks refuge in God ought to have a glimpse of the *Atman* that transcends the body.; and the moment one has a glimpse of the Imperishable *Atman*, one sheds the love of the perishable body. Training in non-violence is therefore diametrically opposed to training in violence. Violence is needed for the protection of things external, non-violence is needed for the protection of the *Atman*, for the protection of one's honour.[13]

To teach the lesson of how to live, the teacher ought to learn the lesson of self-restraint. In this regard, the learners actually become the teachers in leading a life and sharing their habits, manners, approaches and strategies for learning. She/He ought to be an object lesson to them. As Gandhi foresees:

> It is possible for a teacher situated miles away to affect the spirit of the pupils by his way of living. It would be idle for me if I were a liar, to teach boys to tell the truth. A cowardly teacher would never succeed in making his boys valiant, and a stranger to self-restraint. I saw, therefore, that I must be an eternal object-lesson to the boys and girls living with me. They thus become my teacher, and I learnt I must be good and live straight, if only for their sakes. I may say that the increasing discipline and restraint I imposed on myself at Tolstoy Farm was mostly due to those words of mine.[14]

As a practical visionary in meaningful and purposeful education, Gandhi's suggestions on teaching-learning through the mother tongue are always valuable. Today's teacher education definitely needs a wider canvas of teaching and training teachers how to be most justified to education by introducing better strategies of teaching-learning through the mother tongue. In this connection, Gandhi's own experiences and view points are significant:

> I had lost one year because of my marriage, and the teacher wanted me to make good the loss by skipping a class—a privilege usually allowed to industrious boys. I therefore had only six months in the third standard and was promoted to the fourth after the examinations which are followed by the summer vacation. English became the medium of instruction in most subjects from the fourth standard. I found myself completely at sea. Geometry was new subject in which I was not particularly strong, and the English medium made it still more difficult for me. The teacher taught the subject very well, but I could not follow him. Often I would lose heart and think of going back to the third standard, feeling that the packing of two years' studies into a single year was too ambitious.

> If our education were more systematic, and the boys free from the burden of having to learn their subjects through a foreign medium, I am sure learning all these languages would not be an irksome task, but a perfect pleasure. A scientific knowledge of one language makes a knowledge of other languages comparatively easy.[15]

Elsewhere, Gandhi has advised teaching through the mother tongue as a strong foundation in sensitising appropriate teaching-learning:

> India has to flourish in her own climate and scenery and her own literature, even though all the three may be inferior to the English climate, scenery and literature. We and our children must build on our own language. If we borrow another, we impoverish our own. We can never grow on foreign victuals. I want the nation to have the treasures contained in that language, and for that matter in the other languages of the world, through its own vernaculars. I do not need to learn Bengali in order to know the beauties of Rabindranath's matchless productions. I get them through good translations. Gujarati boys and girls do not need to learn Russian to appreciate the Tolstoy's short stories. They learn them through good translations. It is the boast of Englishmen that the best of the world's literary output is in the hands of that nation in simple English inside of a week of its publication. Why need I learn English to get at the best of what Shakespeare and Milton wrote and thought?[16]

Reorientation of teacher education by re-designing our curriculum for teaching-learning for translating the concept of the 'whole man' as Gandhi has envisioned and practised in his own school deserves serious attention right now. As true teaching stands for translating a coherence of diverse developments, the teacher ought to be devoted to imparting 'education of the heart'. Gandhi has clearly spelt out this as follows:

> Take the case of a child in whom the education of the heart is attended to from the very beginning. Supposing he is set to some useful occupation like spinning, carpentry, agriculture etc., for his education and in that connection is given a thorough comprehensive knowledge relating to the theory of the various operations that he is to perform and the use and construction of the tools that he would be wielding. He would not only develop a fine, healthy body but also a sound, vigorous intellect that is not merely academic but is firmly rooted in and is tested from day to day by experience. His

> intellectual education would include a knowledge of mathematics and the various sciences that are useful for an intelligent and efficient exercise of his a-vocation. If to this is added literature by way of recreation, it would give him a perfect, well- balanced, all-round education in which the intellect, the body and the spirit have all full play and develop together into a natural, harmonious whole. Man is neither mere intellect, nor the gross animal body, nor the heart or soul alone. A proper and harmonious combination of all the three is required for the making of the whole man, and constitutes the true economics of education.[17]

The crisis in quality teaching is undeniably the crisis in nation building. It is the crisis that eats up the vitality of a nation and makes it indifferent to the education of the right kind for that of the right mind in a right ambience where the teacher and the learners are in a harmonised and conjoint adventure in teaching and learning. The quest so undertaken is endless. The teacher wants to be as justified to every learner, irrespective of merit and efforts, as best as possible. At the same time, the learners, too, strive for excellence and beyond that ceaselessly. This is not a dream but a living and much desirable reality. The translation of that reality banks heavily upon ardent teachers. In his address to the delegates, who had completed their training in the teaching of crafts, Gandhi's poignant remarks are still relevant:

> What we need is educationists with originality, fired with true zeal, and who will think out from day to day, what they are going to teach their pupils. The teacher can't get this knowledge through the musty volumes. He has to use his own faculties of observation and thinking and impart his knowledge to the children through his lips, with the help of a craft. This means a revolution in the method of teaching, that is, a revolution in the teacher's outlook. Up till now, you have been guided by the inspectors' reports. You wanted to do what the inspector might like, so that you might get more money for your institutions or higher salaries for yourselves. But the new teacher will not care for all that. He will say, 'I have done my duty by my pupil if I

> have made him a better man and in doing so I have used all my resources. That is enough for me.[18]

Gandhi, a pioneer par excellence for best thinking, best living and best translating teaching for fullness and beyond, is an eternal role model for accelerating quality and depth of vision in education.

When would we faithfully follow the footprints of Mahatma Gandhi as an unparalleled visionary in teacher education for quality and excellence?

References

1. *Young India,* 4th August, 1928.
2. Tendulkar, D.G.: *Mahatma,* Publications Division, Ministry of Information and Broadcasting, Government of India, Vol. II, pp. 235-236.
3. *Harijan,* 14th May, 1938.
4. *Harijan,* 25th March, 1939.
5. Pyarelal: *Mahatma Gandhi: The Last Phase,* Navajivan Publishing House, Ahmedabad, 1958, Vol. II, p. 233.
6. Palkhiwala, N.A.: "Relevance of Gandhi Today", *Gandhi Marg,* 61, April 1984. Tenth Gandhi Peace Foundation Lecture on the Martyrs' Day, 30th January, 1984, p. 5.
7. Tendulkar, D.G.: *Mahatma,* Publications Division, Ministry of Information and Broadcasting, Government of India, Vol. III, p. 294.
8. *Young India,* 9th December, 1931.
9. *Harijan,* 9th October, 1937.
10. *From Yeravda Mandir,* Navajivan Publishing House, Ahmedabad, 1935, p. 18.
11. *Report of the First Annual Meeting of the Federation of International Fellowships* held at the Satyagraha Ashram, Sabarmati, 13-15 January, 1928. Published by the Federation of International Fellowships.
12. Desai, Mahadev: *The Diary of Mahadev Desai,* Navajivan Publishing House, Ahmedabad, Vol. I, 1959, p. 188.

13. *Harijan,* September 1st, 1940.
14. *An Autobiography,* Navajivan Publishing House, Ahmedabad, 1927, Chapter XXXIV, p. 249.
15. *Ibid.,* Chapter V, pp. 12-13.
16. *Harijan,* July 9, 1936.
17. *Basic Education,* Navajivan Publishing House, Ahmedabad, 1956, pp. 11-12.
18. Tendulkar, D.G.: *Mahatma,* Publications Division, Ministry of Information and Broadcasting, Government of India, Vol. V, p. 42.

4 Teacher Education and Inter-relativity between Educational Processes and Environment

Education is a matter of eternal enquiry. It welcomes a process congenial, beneficial, relevant, suggestive, reflective, probing and futuristic. If the process of education is fool-proof and scientific, the ends-in-view of every component under its scanner becomes as clear as crystal. This crystallisation becomes natural and spontaneous, challenging and strenuous in accordance with the environment in which it is cultivated. Naturally, the inter-relativity between educational processes and environment acts as a guiding principle in the progress of education.

Any process in education calls forth an activity or a series of activities under the umbrella of an environment. If the environment is congenial and quality-boosting, the process becomes easily apprehensive and motivating. If, on the other hand, the environment betrays a natural and undisturbed climate, the process turns out to be really very difficult and challenging. This does not necessarily indicate that where there is no favourable climate for the exercise of the process of education, there cannot be any advancement of quality and excellence. What is really very challenging and interesting is that the process of education is never static. It is a synchronised one which probes and penetrates, cultures and brings about a radical and evolving platform of environment. In doing so, it reveals newer principles and procedures, methodologies and avenues of implementation so much so that it becomes justified to both in education for quality enhancement and environmental efflorescence.

The process of education is primarily concerned with two kinds of environment—the learning environment and the teaching one. But it must be admitted at the outset that there is essentially no difference between these two kinds of environments because education in the true sense of the term incorporates both as one and the same for fullness, ascent and excellence. In the present system of education for teaching and learning, these become meaningful, purposeful, natural and spontaneous infusion and hardly in separation. These become a single, unified and consolidated process that stands for quality and excellence. Thus, when we say about an environment in education, it always includes the processes of teaching and learning in a conjoint and assimilative manner where the learner and the teacher become a synchronised adventurer in the world of advancement in education.

Bearing in mind the perspective as above of the inter-relativity between the process of education and environment, we might also consider the role of the other components like aesthetics, humanism, spirituality and mysticism, etc., which are closely related to the refinement of both the process and the environment. In fact, these components significantly contribute to education for having, loving and being in sync with the environment for exercise of transfer of evaluation and transfer of values. Truly, all education and, for that end-in-view, the environment look forward to serving as a vital, living, thrilling, challenging and evolving scanner to the cultivation of finer and softer sensibilities for an enlightened environment-local, community-based, societal, state, national or trans-national whatsoever. That the success of any process of education is reflected in the well-being and advancement of the environment immediate or otherwise in terms of harmony in humane relationship is one of the greatest and noblest identities of man the ever unknown.

The intensive preparation for bringing about newer concepts, clarifications, analyses, and appraisals of education in tune with environment is confronted with volleys of askances as follows: Are the processes of education well spelt out in terms of available or likely to be available environment? Are the concerned curricular contents and methodologies duly adhered to or contextual in receiving the right response from the right environment? What about quality in teaching? How do learners play their role? What about infrastructure and teaching-learning facilities? What are the prospects for innovative exercises? What contribution does the process of education under continual and critical scanner provide for an attractive, refined and serene environment?

Teacher education in the twenty-first century is absolutely aware of the desirable dynamics of teacher-preparation for assuring and accelerating enlightened and humane environment. Recently, the Right to Children to Free and Compulsory Education Act has set forth the process of education and environment under an umbrella of dedicated and wholehearted devotion to the role of the teacher who ought to be justified to the inter-relativity between the process of education and environment. As the National Curriculum Framework for Teacher Education (NCFTE) reminds us:

> The teacher must be equipped not only to teach but also to understand the students and the community of parents so that children are regular in schools and learn. The Act mandates that the teacher should refrain from inflicting corporal punishment, complete the entire curriculum within the given time, assess students, hold parent's meetings and apprise them and as part of the school management committee organise the overall running of the school. (Right of Children to Free and Compulsory Education Act, 2009. The Gazette of India, August 27, 2009, New Delhi, p. 9).

The Act, *vide* Section 29(2), emphasises the following areas while laying down the curriculum and evaluation procedures:

- Conformity with the values enshrined in the Constitution.
- All round development of the child.
- Building up child's knowledge, potentiality and talent.
- Development of physical and mental abilities to the fullest extent.
- Learning through activities, discovery and exploration in a child-friendly and child-centred manner.
- Medium of instruction shall, as far as practicable, be in child's mother tongue.
- Making the child free of fear, trauma and anxiety and helping the child to express views freely.

- Comprehensive and continuous evaluation of child's understanding of knowledge and his or her ability to apply the same.

These areas are particularly significant to the professional development of teachers at all stages, both in their initial and in-service training.

> In addition, the NCF requires a teacher to be a facilitator of children's learning in a manner that helps children to construct knowledge and meaning. The teacher in this process is a co-constructor of knowledge. It also opens out possibilities for the teacher to participate in the construction of syllabi, textbooks and teaching-learning materials. Such roles demand that teachers be equipped with an adequate understanding of curriculum, subject-content and pedagogy, on the one hand, and the community and school structures and management, on the other.[1]

Designing and building an enviable platform of cohesive and challenging environment calls forth sustained endeavour in refinement of the process of education. The teacher ought to explore and accommodate all possibilities for broadening the mission and vision of the learner in a prospective environment where the seeds of intellectual, social, cultural, economic, moral, aesthetic, spiritual and humanistic efflorescence of personality are nurtured in an environment of freedom and joy. Let the process of education be so fine tuned with the spirit of the exercise of inherent feelings under a cordial and communicative environment which will definitely assure newer promises in the very moderation of our processes of education which would ward off transitory constraints in the advancement and excellence from diverse dimensions.

Education policies in strengthening and disseminating the appropriate and characteristic climate of consciousness for a really positive and education-savvy optimistic environment should be justified with both long-term and short-term plans and programmes of action. Unfortunately, we are yet to satisfactorily remodel our process of education that is justified to the environment in terms of representation of the aspirations of a whole community of humane relationship with the spirit of pluralism and generous partnership of knowledge and experience, skills and values, equity and quality, socio-aesthetics and cross-cultural ambience of empathy and togetherness. The formal education system, therefore, necessitates an overall regulation. As the Delors Commission categorically advocates:

> Education policies must be long-term instruments, presupposing continuity of choices made and in the implementation of reforms. In the field of education, it is important to rise above short-term responses or reforms one after another that risk being reversed at the next change of government. Long-term planning should be based on in-depth analysis of reality (accurate diagnoses, forward analysis, social and economic background information, awareness of world education trends and assessment of results).
>
> These are the main justifications for the role of the state, as representative of the whole community, in a pluralistic and partnership-based society where education is a life-time affair. That role relates mainly to the social choices that set their mark on education, but also to the regulation of the system as a whole and to the promotion of the value of education; it must not, however, be exercised as a strict monopoly. It is more a matter of channelling energies, promoting initiatives and providing the conditions in which new synergies can emerge. It is also a matter of insisting on equity and quality in education. The principles of equity and the right to education require, at the very least, that access to education should not be denied to certain persons or social groups; more specifically, the state should play a redistributive role, to the benefit of minorities and the underprivileged especially. Guaranteeing educational quality moreover implies the establishment of general standards and various monitoring devices.[2]

The challenges of the process of education best suited to the needs and priorities of the environment are legion. It must cater to community participation and responsibilities whereby the ambience is proactive to sensitise values amongst all the members of the community in an environment where confusions and contradictions are sincerely and steadfastly replaced by shouldering all assignments shared and substantiated by the local community in harmony with the ongoing and stimulating processes of education for an enlightened and healthy change. The processes of education should always invite revaluation of the concerned environment in terms of intensive care and reflection. The very success of schooling should be geared by a thorough and error-free freedom and vigour in environmental awareness which is all the time backed by a living and radical process of education for community involvement. As the Report to UNESCO of the International Commission on Education for the twenty-first century appositely suggests:

> The success of schooling depends in very large measure upon the value that communities attach to education. Where education is highly valued and actively sought, the mission and goals of the school are shared and supported by the community. Thus, the increasing focus on the role of local communities needs to be encouraged and supported. Education needs to be seen by the community as applicable to their real-life situations, needs and aspirations. Specific characteristics of life in both rural and urban environments should be taken into account, through decisions about the language of instruction and a careful analysis of what needs to be adapted in the curriculum, course content, teacher training and materials. Where there is reluctance on the part of parents to send their children to school, involving the local community in the assessment of needs— through a dialogue with the authorities and other interested groups within society, and a continuation of that dialogue through use of the media, community discussions, parental education and training-can result in the community assuming greater responsibility for its own welfare and development.[3]

The processes of education should respond to nurturing an enabling environment where the world of education becomes the learner's own, very endearingly and supportively own. It should be an ideal environment of teaching-learning where both the teacher and the learner enjoy and appreciate in cohesion the quest for efflorescence, quality and excellence. As the National Curriculum Framework 2005 suggests:

> An enabling learning environment is one where children feel secure, where there is absence of fear, and which is governed by relationships of equality and equity. Often this does not require any special effort on the part of the teacher, except to practise equality and not discriminate among children. Teachers should also nurture their classroom spaces as places where children can ask questions freely, engaging in a dialogue with the teacher as well as their peers, during an ongoing lesson. Unless they can share their related experiences, clarify their doubts and ask questions, they will not engage with learning. If, instead of ignoring children's comments or sealing their tongues with strict rules of silence and restrictions on the language to be used, teachers encourage children to talk, they would find that the classroom is a more lively place and that teaching is not predictable and boring, but rather an adventure of interacting minds. Such an environment will facilitate the self-confidence and self-esteem of learners of all ages; it will also go a long way in improving the quality of learning itself.[4]

In an era of introducing the processes of education for radical change in embracing a thriving and energising environment, a far deeper role of the teachers in rethinking what is to be taught, why and when would definitely work wonders. Classroom learning and teaching should be extended to a global environment in a natural and distinctive policy perspective where the very concepts of both processes of education and 'Information Superhighway' are in worthwhile unison. In the invaluable words of Professor Scrimshaw:

> If we look beyond the classroom and the school we see a world in which changes are continuous and diverse. Historically, schools have been partly sheltered from these processes, because in their location, staffing and to some extent in the knowledge they were expected to transmit they were physically and organisationally separate from the society around them. But all these three screens between schools and society are, for good or ill, disintegrating, making schools far more open to external influences. This opens up another route by which computers will influence teaching and learning, because society

> itself is being powerfully and directly changed by the ways in which computers are being employed.[5]

Human ecology, one of the essential ends-in-view of human development needs identification in terms of its role in education for human development under a favourable climate of quality acceleration. As regards the concept human ecology which holds the key to education under a positive climate of advancement, the following needs attention in relation to economic ecology:

> Human ecology, in essence, means the creation of essential conditions to every human being for assuring him a healthy, creative and productive life, under equal opportunity and an equitable order, where the aptitudes and desires can develop and be fulfilled in the normal and humanistic way. The satisfaction of the basic material and non-material needs for each human being at equitable level stands at the very foundation of the concept of human ecology.
>
> Economic ecology is the concept of human needs-based development of natural and human resources and sources, utilisation and processing of the same in such a rationalised way as not to meet the end in humanely non-productive way. It presupposes the adjustment of the economic factorial input and output in such a way as to meet the humankind's productive needs. Both the renewable and non-renewable materials are to be used only to the level of human survival or maintenance and its productive human developmental values. Therefore, the utilisation motivation of human resources, natural resource, capital and credit, technology and the organisational function, has to be guided by the desire of the creation of human-use values and their exchange functions are also to be organised on the premises of human values. In other words, the function of capital, technology and entrepreneur is to be harmonised and this is the essence of human ecology.[6]

For a renewal of values in education for environmental awareness, teacher education cannot but give priorities to the advancement of training and orientation of student-teachers and freshers in some of the fundamental areas of human ecology and economic ecology. A major paradigm shift from materialistic and figure-happy statistical pointers to education to living, genuine, sensitised and meaningful education for the purpose of creating and maintaining a balanced relationship between socio-humanistic and all embracing education for one and all is right now necessary.

The twenty-first teacher education scenario is to be well aware of the emerging needs of social and humane development in terms of the much debated issues of sustainability and developmental crises writ large in our plans and programmes of curricular and co-curricular activities in connection with teacher proficiency and teacher enrichment in the specialised zones of appropriate resources for maintenance of a balanced and crystallised process of enlightened excellence. At the same time, let us open-heartedly accept the fact that in teacher education much more homework is required in reframing the curriculum at every stage of teacher education for bridging the challenging gaps between educational processes and environmental awareness. In this connection, the following might serve as a forewarning:

> Since sustainable development is the cry and much-talked issue of the day, put forward as an effective social and development alternative, let us concentrate on the means and methods of realising the same. Such type of developments is to be organised at the local level with local human and material means and resources, as far as possible, and with appropriate techno-methodology, with a view to solving the local problems and serving local community. The guided development or development from above, as practised in the state capitalised socialised economics, should be avoided, because the homogenisation process from above cannot produce the appropriate economic and social order at the bottom. In this respect, certain failures of wrong applications are also to be taken into account for the purpose of learning appropriate lessons. The Gandhian concept of village socialism was never tried in India while the Tanzanian experiment of socialism, as conceived in the Arusha Declaration, did fail, Mao's Commune

> socialism and Kim II-Sung's Jucche socialism also proved to be unsuccessful. And, finally, the East European system has completely and chaotically collapsed. The only lesson one may learn from the above in the homogenisation process from about with the absence of participation from below can never succeed.[7]

Education of the heart in perfect tune with education of the head is long overdue in our process of education for environmental ascent and excellence. Only the ever alert mind-set is the most positive alternative.

Do we believe?

References

1. *National Council for Teacher Education: Towards Preparing Professional and Humane Teacher,* National Council for Teacher Education, New Delhi, 2009, pp. 2-3.
2. *Learning: A Treasure Within,* Report to UNESCO of the International Commission on Education for the Twenty-first Century, UNESCO, 1996, pp. 161-162.
3. *Ibid.,* pp. 122-123.
4. *National Curriculum Framework 2005,* National Council of Educational Research and Training, New Delhi, 2005, pp. 81-82.
5. Scrimshaw, Peter: "Computers and the Teacher's Role", *Knowledge, Power and Learning,* (Ed. Carrie Paechter *et al*), Paul Chapman Publishing Limited, London, 2001, p. 142.
6. Guha, Amalendu: "Human Ecology and Economic Ecology: Two Important Aspects of Development Alternatives for the 21st Century", *Development and Human Ecology,* Institute for Alternative Development Research, Oslo, Norway, 1997, p. 9.
7. *Ibid.,* p. 142.

5 Teacher Education and School-internship: A Quest for Quality-enrichment

Teacher education for its quality and excellence depends a great deal on its skillful and appropriate handling of practice in teaching. It is one of the best ways for every teacher trainee or a fresher in the training of teaching to exercise every lesson to be taught now or in the future so that whatever she/he has theoretically learnt in the course of attending any teachers' training institution to which she/he is attached becomes living and useful. Moreover, the role of the teacher in the classroom ought to be justified by means of continual and earnest practice in every lesson much before her/his actual assignment in teaching in an institution where she/he would serve as a teacher.

Keeping in the right perspective the importance of practice in teaching as above, school internship has become one of the major areas of importance in teacher education. The integration between general education and school education by means of school internship is the surest avenue of professional development in teaching. As such, priorities should be given to internship for student teachers in schools for a stipulated period during the training session introduced by any institution for teacher education. As the National Council for Teacher Education suggests, there should be a compulsory schedule of activities for student teachers under school internship as follows:

1. Four days in a week for a minimum period of 12-20 weeks including one week of classroom observation of a regular teacher.
2. Visit to Innovative Centres of Pedagogy and Learning.
3. Classroom Research and Development of Learning Resources.

Apart from the above, in the initial and in-service training of teachers should have a primary and obligatory end-in-view of fulfilling the vision of education in terms of curriculum and evaluation procedures as declared in Section 29 (2) in the Right of Children to Free and Compulsory Education Act, 2009.

- Conformity with the values enshrined in the Constitution.
- All round development of the child.
- Building up child's knowledge, potentiality and talent.
- Development of physical and mental abilities to the fullest extent.
- Learning through activities, discovery and exploration in a child-friendly and child-centred manner.
- Medium of instruction shall, as far as practicable, be in the child's mother tongue.
- Making the child free of fear, trauma and anxiety and helping the child to express views freely.
- Comprehensive and continuous evaluation of the child's understanding of knowledge and his or her ability to apply the same.

Understanding the community life of students, parental role for the education of children and taking an active, positive, sincere and living interest in the advancement of quality education for students irrespective of caste, creed, sex, parental upbringing and so on are some of the most crucial challenges of teaching and teacher education. Today's teacher is not simply a task master but a learner first before being a teacher especially of children in schools. This is also the most significant and important in rural schools in our country where the learners and their parents/guardians suffer from numerous and serious academic constraints, social and other limitations notwithstanding.

Meanwhile with the appalling mushroom growth of sub-standard educational institutions, the basic learning needs are ignored and quality education is hardly available due to paucity of adequate and properly trained teachers who sincerely believe that teaching is not a mechanical and information-happy activity but a conjoint and ardently reciprocal endeavour between each learner and the teacher as co-constructors in quest of reflective teaching-learning. Indeed, it is a harmonious and well-balanced activity where no compromise is allowed in the arena of quality and excellence. It is time to understand, emphasise and disseminate the fact that teaching must be a sincere, devoted and dedicated occupation and should never be a casual, fleeing and non-preferential option.

As regards teacher education curriculum reform in relation to quality and excellence in teaching, the current problems of teacher education as highlighted in the National Curriculum Framework, 2005 necessitates our immediate attention:

- Experiences in the practice of teacher education indicate that knowledge is treated as 'given', embedded in the curriculum and accepted without question; there is no engagement with the curriculum. Curriculum, syllabi and textbooks are never critically examined by the student teacher or the regular teacher.
- Language proficiency of the teacher needs to be enhanced, but existing programmes do not recognise the centrality of language in the curriculum.
- Teacher education programmes provide little scope for student teachers to reflect on their experiences.
- Disciplinary knowledge is viewed as independent of professional training in pedagogy.
- Repeated 'practice' in the teaching of a specified number of isolated lessons is considered a sufficient condition for professional development.
- It is assumed that links between learning theories and models and teaching methods are automatically formed in the understanding developed by student teachers.

- There is no opportunity for teachers to examine their own biases and beliefs and reflect on their own experiences as part of the classroom discourse and enquiry.
- Theory courses have no clear link with practical work and ground realities.
- The evaluation system followed in teacher education programmes is too information-oriented, excessively quantitative and lacks comprehensiveness.
- Apart from conceptual and pedagogical aspects, existing programmes need to develop certain attitudes, dispositions, habits and interests in a teacher. The present evaluation protocol has no place for evaluating these aspects.

—*National Curriculum Framework for Teacher Education: Towards Preparing Professional and Humane Teacher,* National Council for Teacher Education, New Delhi, 2009, pp. 11-12.

School-internship, from the viewpoints apart as above, also carries forth a new vision of teacher education for a radical change in the approach to teaching not merely from the reflective, creative, alternative and radical points of view but also brightens the possibilities of positive teaching where learning to be as one of the most characteristic pillars of education is based and nurtured on a strong foundation. The student teachers in association with regular teachers become continual learners in different branches of knowledge and experience shared and contributed in the vibrant classroom and outside the classrooms with learners. Indeed teaching becomes an endless adventure in the world of teaching-learning where the bond of humane relationship is spontaneously strengthened.

Teacher education and student internship are closely related to two very essential ends-in-view towards which effective teaching is directed. One of these is clarity, and the other is patience on the part of a student-teacher or a regular teacher. The role of the teacher educator is to continually remind the student teacher under school internship during the live teaching practice session how to be justified to the best of her/his abilities to clarity and patience, the two significant components which amply contribute to successful teaching. As Professor Highet advises:

> Whenever you are teaching, make it clear. Make it as firm as stone and as bright as sunlight. Not to yourself—that is easy. Make it clear to the pupil you are teaching—that is difficult. The difficulty lies partly in subject-matter, and partly in language. You must think, not what, what you know, but what they do not know; not what you find hard, but what they will find hard; then, after putting yourself inside their minds, obstinate or puzzled, groping or mistaken as they are, explain what they need to learn. And you must be sure they understand your words. A strange name, a phrase only vaguely understood, will blur an explanation badly. Abstract words mean little on first hearing. Illustrate them. Give pictures and examples. And whenever possible, make sure you have been understood, by talking over what you have been trying to teach. A good pupil is seldom silent.
>
> The second is patience. Anything worth takes time to learn, and time to teach. It is a mistake often made by great scholars and distinguished statesmen, to assume that their audiences have thought deeply about their problems are only a few steps behind them in any discussion—so that they treat as partially solved problems which the majority of their audience have scarcely envisaged, or dart rapidly from one obscure question to another without attempting to show the connection. Real teaching is not handing out packages of information. It culminates in a conversation, an actual change of the pupil's mind. An important change takes a long time to carry through, and should therefore be planned carefully and approached in slow stages with plenty of repetition disguised by variation. It is particularly important to keep out emotion, or rather to control it carefully.[1]

In student internship introduced and designed for improvement of quality in teaching, the fundamental points of interest are:

(a) To enable the student teacher to exercise the different skills of teaching in a heterogeneous and macro classroom situation.

(b) To stimulate the student teacher to be active and positive in creating a congenial and interesting classroom atmosphere in dealing with the different teaching components in close and sincere participation of learners.

(c) To equip the student teacher in the appropriate application of different aids in teaching where innovative teaching-learning situation is favourably created in close and active participation of learners.

(d) To enable the student teacher to be enriched with the suggestions put forward by the regular teachers of the practising institutions during their period of observations of teaching practice.

(e) To encourage the student teacher to receive the comments from learners to individually fill in the Teacher Assessment Proforma already supplied to or prepared by the latter and orient future strategies for effective teaching in a more pinpointed and error-free way after an intensive and thorough study of their comments.

(f) To encourage the student teacher to carefully assess the comments received from learners and re-plan the lesson accordingly in order to ascertain how far she/he as a student teacher is justified to the re-teaching session.

Needless to say, the above strategies for improvement in teaching is essentially geared to provoking critical thinking and creative reflection on practice. The critical lenses applied or used are meant for four types of identification encompassing the student teacher who is otherwise named as the teaching practitioner, the learner pupils who are otherwise identified as the classroom partner in teaching practice, the teaching problem, lesson-item, topic or point-matter or subject-matter, and the observers, mentors, peer-attendants or classmates as associated student-teachers (Fig. 1).

It is interesting to note that a great deal of reflective teaching is covered under the active participation of all these under the critical lenses. Besides the technical aspects under teaching sessions the whole academic activities are under critical scanner which also assist in deeper reflection needed for effective quality teaching. As Professor Harrison elucidates:

Thinking about reflective practice as a concept is crucial since we do need to be clear about what it means. Whether we are

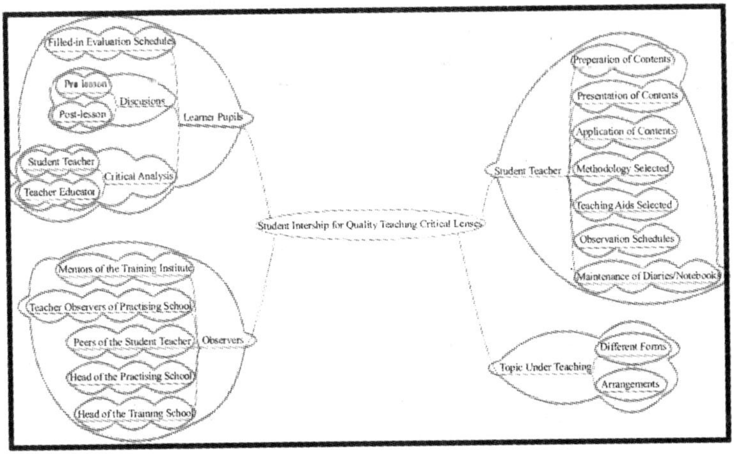

Fig. 1.

beginning teachers, university education tutors or school mentors involved in school-based training, it is important that all of us have a chance to clarify what we understand by it and what we expect it to entail. Our starting point is that it is much more than just thinking about teaching. It can be thought about in terms of asking searching questions about experience and conceptualised as both a state of mind and an on-going type of behaviour. Zeichner and Liston (1996) provide a helpful overview of the traditions of reflective teaching. Being a reflective practitioner at any stage in teacher development involves a constant, critical look at teaching and learning and at the work of you, the teacher.

Reflecting on aspects of teaching practice is usually fairly instinctive for most beginning teachers. You will focus mentally on particular problems or dilemmas that are to do with how a particular teaching session went. Often, perhaps with the aid of a lesson evaluation form, you will identify what went well during the teaching session, and what did not go according to plan. You will then be encouraged to go on to think about what might need changing in the next teaching session, or to

> identify what could be tried out in other types of teaching sessions. This takes you from an essentially technical kind of reflection towards a more practical level, in which you begin to examine the interpretative assumptions you are making in your work.[2]

For professional enrichment through school internship, student teachers in course of their reflective teaching practice might record significant and critical moments. These records are normally maintained not only for improvements of future class-room assignments but also directed towards case studies for teaching and research. Moreover, the learners contribute a lot to extend their cooperation in group discussions during the post-teaching sessions. Indeed, quality improvement and acceleration by means of school internship become more comprehensive, meaningful and transparent through reflective teaching cases under the five-fold scanner of observation, communication, judgement, decision-making and team-working. To encourage student teachers to inspire learners in critical reflection, the suggestions of Professor Harrison are essentially directed towards attaining excellence in teaching:

> One frequently used activity in teacher training programmes to encourage reflection is the use of reflective writing assignments. These allow you to draw from and enlarge upon examples of the critical moments which you might have recorded in your journal or diary. Sometimes these reflective assignments might involve the writing and analysing of a teaching case. You could be asked to identify a dilemma you are experiencing in the classroom and write a narrative or story about this event or situation. Its intention is to help you highlight the complexity of problem-solving and decision-making in learning and teaching. It also provides a way of observing and analysing your own teaching, rather than relying on relatively infrequent observations by others. Another purpose is to help you uncover beliefs and assumptions about teaching.
>
> Written case study accounts such as these might then be shared with others through a case conference. This allows collaborative analysis and discussion about the case. A group

> of beginning teachers reflects together on the embedded dilemmas, identifies the range of possible solutions and, in so doing, each can relate another's case to their own teaching experience. There is some research evidence (Lundeberg and Scheurman, 1997) to show that beginning teachers do benefit from a second reading of a case analysis in that it helps them connect theoretical knowledge with practice.
>
> Another possibility is for you to stop a moment and step into another person's shoes (for example, a student, parent, social worker) and consider how that person's perspective might be different from your own. What differences might there be? How does knowing about the differences change your own perspective on a situation or event? In this way you can start to consider the role of race, class, ethnicity and gender with regard to teaching dilemmas.[3]

The importance of keeping a reflective journal by every intern student teacher is legion. It serves as a pointer to positive and quality teaching in future. As the NCFTE advises:

> Each intern would be expected to keep a reflective journal that would help him/her revisit his/her experiences in the classroom over the period of internship. The journal would include short descriptions of how the class was conducted, how learners responded, followed by analytical and reflective statements about his/her preparedness for the class, responses to the learners' questions, capacity to include learners' sharing of their experiences, response towards their errors, difficulties in comprehending new ideas and concepts and issues of discipline, organisation and management of the group, individual and whole class activities. Evaluation of the journal would mean looking at how the intern has been able to gradually move towards writing reflections rather than merely describing class-room events and processes.[4]

Admittedly, teaching dilemmas are boons to student teachers because they rediscover themselves as excellent practitioners through SWOT analysis by means of self-observation where their strengths, weaknesses, opportunities and threats are further crystallised in course of discussions on the problems and challenges arising out of learner inputs already recorded with care.

The following (Fig. 2) shows how the post-teaching discussions with learners and their suggestions as reflective learners pave further ways of excellence in reflective teaching by means of reviews received from mentors and teacher educators:

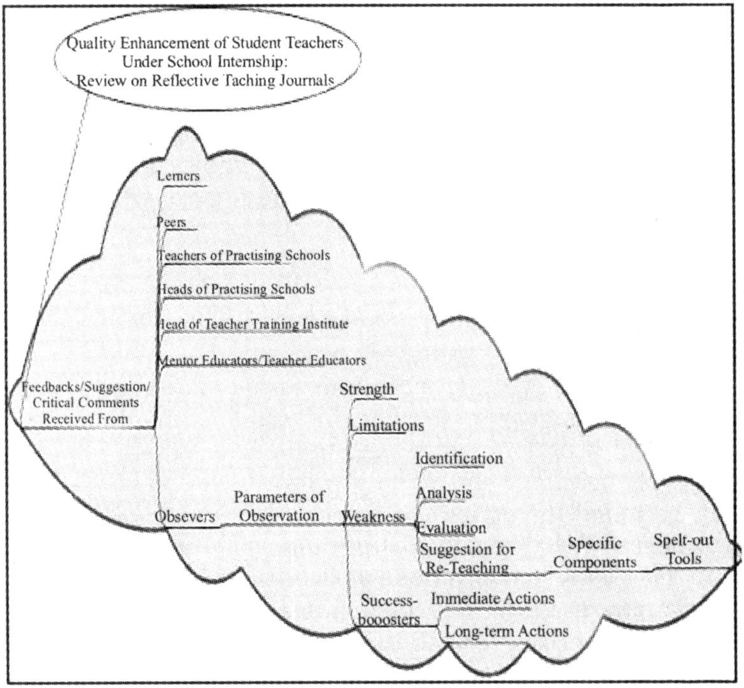

Fig. 2.

The vision of the role of the teacher needs more transparency in the light of what true teaching means as a reflector of creative and critical thinking. Mere doling out some teaching items in the classroom will simply be boring to the learners as they do not find any impetus to go ahead with their own patterns of learning to think and learning to be. School internship is a practical means to be radical and innovative in the student teachers' approaches to teaching. As such, the best ideas, best feelings, best reflective strategies and best outcomes of teaching learning should always come under the purview of school internship. As the NCFTE categorically asserts:

> It is obvious that in imparting professional rigour to the preparation of a teacher, the practice of teaching and associated rigorous theoretical study play a crucial part. It is the effectiveness with which the multiple components of field learning—getting to know the school, observing children, observing teaching and learning in real classroom contexts, practising teaching, developing capacities to think with educational theories and applying concepts in concrete teaching-learning situations, managing classroom learning, evaluating learners and providing feedback, learning to work with colleagues, reflecting on one's own professional practice—are drawn upon to provide appropriate learning experiences for the study of the student teacher that is critical to the education of teachers.
>
> At the outset, it can be seen that any attempt towards reform of current practices and design of innovative approaches in practice teaching should begin with an understanding of the place of teaching practice in the overall scheme of things. The first thing to be noted is that the practice of teaching constitutes the hub of the multiple and varied activities comprising the total programme of teacher education. It is inter-connected with theoretical study, field work and practicum and a wide range of institutional experiences involving school students, teachers, student teachers, mentor teacher educators. In a way, it acts both as the evaluation tool for effective teacher education as well as its critical quality indicator. [5]

School internship is yet to be given its proper role either in student teacher preparation in general and enrichment in teacher education in particular. At the same time, community awareness for quality teaching-learning is still at a low ebb. Parents and guardians, let us frankly admit, do not take particular interest in fostering student teachers' devoted activities in or outside the classroom or in parent-teachers' or other allied meetings by means of holding cordial platforms for discussions on how to mutually contribute best to the advancement of teaching-learning. Again, if a few practical suggestions arrived at through joint discussions among the members of the teaching staff of the school under internship and the school internee teacher students be utilised for quality enhancement after due moderation by the teacher educators and other mentors, the school climate becomes more attractive, fascinating, participatory, intensive, qualitative and meaningful as a serene cathedral of education.

The rationale of teacher trainees is yet to be clarified in terms of contemporary teaching-learning. Mere doling out a few lessons just to be rest assured with the fulfilment of quota or the prescribed number of classes for the purpose of training in teaching through practice is not enough. Reaching the ends-in-view in teaching requires endless preparation, analysis, discussion, evaluation and resetting teaching sessions where the whole canvas of activities calls forth sustained and reflective involvement. As teaching should never be mechanical, dull, dry, drab or drudgery-prone, alert care should be taken to appropriately incorporate any learning aid for the learner lest it destroys the latter's creative and critical spirit of self-learning through self-activity through self-involvement and self-appreciation. This is all the more important for the student teacher or the teacher trainee because she/he might have the tendency to somehow complete the assignments of practice teaching without caring for teaching for the efflorescence of learners' freedom and joy in learning by means of the inspiring and spontaneous exercise of individuality. If the teacher student does not exercise her/his insight for the purpose of vibrant teaching, the purpose of introducing student internship appallingly fails.

As a reminder to the facts stated above, the spelling out of the rationale of student internship as made in the NCFTE 2009 is right now very significant:

> Teacher trainees need to study issues related to self and identity, human relationships, adult-child gaps, assumptions, beliefs and attitudes. They could explore the meaning of ethics and values, observe and understand feelings of fear and trust and their influences in personal and social attitude, attitudes

> towards competition and co-operation, analyse and observe the impact of competition in personal and social life, observe the role of listening, attention and empathy and the role of a teacher in establishing relationship with children and as a communicator. A greater insight into one's aim of life, one's strengths and weaknesses and the dynamics of identity formation provides the base for developing a professionally competent teacher who is sensitive to issues of equity, democracy and social justice.[6]

Student internship in the second decade of the twenty-first century has attained a great deal of importance as it calls forth awareness to human and child rights. The Constitutional provision for reservation and right to education almost entirely banks upon the school climate where institutional, community, social, national and global perspectives of human and child rights are carefully nurtured. To be assured of maintaining a favourable classroom ambience for the exercise and protection of child rights, one or two classes should be particularly earmarked for lessons dealing with equity, gender, culture, poverty, values and freedom to be as incomparable individuals. The lesson plans encapsulated with interesting ideas and concepts in association with the above should be prepared by the student teachers or teacher trainees and these, after thorough check and due approval by the concerned teacher educator, should form a part of the total teaching assignments during the period of intensive school internship.

As an assignment of co-curricular activities, student teachers under school internship might associate themselves with dramatic, musical and other functions and festivals where the images of the pluralistic society, culture, religion, values and soon become living and thrilling to children right from the school stage. The pedagogic processes also undergo interesting and appealing changes for highlighting to the child learners love, patriotism, unity, tolerance, sympathy, solidarity, equity and many other values of conjoint and lively relationship with one and all.

These apart, student teachers during their period of school intership might undertake school-based projects emphasising on the right to education and the right to be grown up as world citizens. With revolution in electronic and computer technology, the world has come nearest to home, school, class, community, the nation and the world. The trainee teacher should always be prepared to enable the learner to be characteristic contributor to education that, that shines in the aura of teaching learning in a perfect fusion of advancement and fostering of individuality. That a student teacher or a teacher trainee learns many more matters of interest from the child learner than learning by herself/himself how to teach is a new focus of child education for protection and enrichment of child right and advancement in newer directions of humane excellence.

Teacher education for school internship right now requires a total overhauling in its approach and parameters of practice. Learning must be well-cohered with teaching. Knowledge must be creation-in-quest and not crushed in crudities of informatics. Wisdom must be the prime end-in-view of teaching-learning that gives us the power to be as one ought to be. Let us be forewarned in teacher education and school internship with the ever worthwhile words of Swami Vivekananda:

> What is education? Is it book-learning? No. is it diverse knowledge? Not even that. The training by which the current and expression of will are brought under control and become fruitful is called education. Now consider, is that education as a result of which the will, being continuously choked by force through generations, is well neigh killed out; is that education under whose sway even the old ideas, let alone the new ones, are disappearing one by one; is that education which is slowly making man a machine? It is more blessed, in my opinion, even to go wrong, impelled by one's free will and intelligence than to be good as an automation. Again, can that be called society which is formed by an aggregate of men who are like lumps of clay, like lifeless machines, like heaped up pebbles? How can such society fare well? Were good possible, then instead of being slaves for hundreds of years, we would have been the greatest nation on earth, and this soil of India, instead of being a mine of stupidity, would have been the eternal fountain-head of learning.[7]

References

1. Gilbert Highet: *The Art of Teaching,* University Paperbacks, Methuen, London, 1963, 246-247.
2. Jennifer Harrison: "Professional Development and the Reflective Practitioner", *Reflective Teaching and Learning* (Sue Dymoke and Jennifer Harrison Ed.), Sage, South Asia Edition, 2010, p. 8.
3. *Ibid.,* pp. 23-24.
4. National *Curriculum Framework for Teacher Education: Towards Preparing Professional and Humane Teacher,* National Council for Teacher Education, New Delhi, 2009, p. 61.
5. *Ibid.,* pp. 40-41.
6. *Ibid.,* p. 33.
7. Swami Vivekananda: *The Complete Works of Swami Vivekananda,* Advaita Ashrama, Kolkata, Mayavati Memorial Edition, 1989, Vol. IV, p. 490.

6 Teacher Education and Professional Development of Teacher Educators: A Quest for Excellence

Teacher education today is undergoing rapid scanning. This has been further aggravated due to unprecedented response from at least three quarters. First, teachers under orientation or training feel that there should be an overhauling in respect of the duties and responsibilities of teacher educators. Second, the quest for quality and excellence in teacher education should primarily be in terms of the axiology of teaching where aesthetics should play a very vital role in teaching for reflective thinking. Third, a positive approach to teacher education should be comprehensively integrated to what the teacher educators in every discipline mould, mediate and moderate the viewpoints and suggestions received immediately from the teacher-trainees or others directly or indirectly associated with teaching as a profession.

In keeping with the scanning scenario as above, teacher education cannot but be responsive to the present day needs and priorities of changes in the development of teachers where teacher educators look forward to having their own skills, interests, attitudes, aptitudes, motivational stylistics and appreciation under continuous response to the educational ends-in-view in perfect accord to the processes and practices carried out in educational institutions. Therefore, a corresponding change in the professional development of teacher educators should, as suggested by the National Council for Teacher Education, cater to the role of the teacher educators who:

- Engage would-be teachers with the larger socio-political context in which education and learners are situated, engage them with children in real contexts than teach them about children through theories, focus on the developmental aspects of children with constant reference to their socio-economic and cultural contexts.
- Bring into the teacher education curriculum and discourse trainees' own assumptions about children and beliefs about knowledge and processes of learning, help teachers to reflect upon their own positions in society-gender, caste, class, poverty, linguistic and regional variation, community, equity and justice.
- Engage with theory along with field experiences to help trainees to view knowledge not as external to the learner but as something that is actively constructed during training, integrate academic knowledge and professional learning into a meaningful whole.
- Provide opportunity for trainees for reflection and independent study without packing the training schedule with teacher directed activities, provide opportunities to the student teacher to critically examine curriculum, syllabi and textbooks.
- View knowledge not as an external reality embedded in textbooks but as constructed in the shared context of teaching-learning and personal experience, change perception of the child as a receiver of knowledge, view learning as a search for meaning out of personal experiences and knowledge generation as a continuously evolving process of reflective learning.[1]

Admittedly, the new vision of teacher education and, for that end-in-view, teacher educators incorporates newer challenges where the role of would be teachers entirely depends on how their teacher educators respond to their radical, reflective and evolving processes of thinking and activities in accordance with the changing needs of the society, and how the latest trends and techniques of education are disseminated and translated into an interesting and thrilling reality. The focus of attention on the part of every teacher educator is to train and orient teacher trainees and freshers in such a way as to create an atmosphere of teaching learning best suited to young learners in every institution everywhere. Away from arbitrary education and make teaching that allows the learner to learn from her/his own enriched world of freedom, creativity, critical awareness and joy. It is time to realise that the professional development of teacher educators entirely depends on how they are justified to orient or train teachers with the supreme devotion to teaching as a quest for education for self-identity and self-development. In this connection, education of the child as Sri Aurobindo advocates ought to be the best guideline:

> The discovery that education must be a bringing out of the child's own intellectual and moral capacities to their highest possible value and must be based on the psychology of the child-nature was a step forward towards a more healthy because a more subjective system; but it still fell short because it still regarded him as an object to be handled and moulded by the teacher, to be educated. But at least there was a glimmering of the realisation that each human being is a self-developing soul and that the business of both parent and teacher is to enable and to help the child to educate himself, to develop his own intellectual, moral, aesthetic and practical capacities and to grow freely as an organic being, not to be kneaded and pressured into form like an inert plastic material. It is not yet realised what this soul is or that the true secret, whether with child or man, is to help him to find his deeper self, the real psychic entity within. That, if we ever give it a chance to come forward, and still more if we call it into the foreground as "the leader of the march set in our front," will itself take up most of the business of education out of our hands and develop the capacity of the psychological being towards a realisation of potentialities of which our present mechanical view of life and man and external routine methods of dealing with them prevent us from having any experience or forming any conception. These new educational methods are on the straight way to this truer dealing. The closer touch attempted with the psychical entity behind the vital and physical mentality and an increasing reliance on its possibilities must lead to the ultimate discovery that man is inwardly a soul and a conscious power of the divine and that the evocation of this real man within is the right object of education and indeed of all human life if it would find and

live according to the hidden Truth and deepest law of its own being.[2]

To prepare teacher educators in tune with the ends-in-view of education as above is really a very challenging task. As the teacher-trainees look forward to exploring a path-breaking and altogether fresh approach to education, teacher education should primarily be geared to the purpose of involving every teacher educator in undertaking an adventure in teaching-learning where a conjoint and well-communicated strategy of finding out the soul of teaching which indeed is the teaching of inwardness and being becomes the most essential assignment for the culture of education for all encompassing consciousness and beyond that for the quest unending, unparalleled and incomparable.

Truly, professional development of teacher education fundamentally depends on the role of teacher educators who are not only educators of teachers or would-be teachers under teachers' training programmes but also a role model for what teaching in the real sense of the term stands for. She/He sensitises the different strategies, methodologies, policies, perspectives, nuances, stylistics, ideas, criticisms, emotions, impulses, and various other inner movements keeping in view her/his own standpoints alert but apart so much so that teaching becomes an add-on and stimulating affair in the vast and multi-dimensional arena of teaching learning. She/he becomes so involved as to safeguard herself/himself with the extinction of personality as best as possible which leaves a permanent impression on every one of her/his learners undergoing training in teaching, who, again, modifies, crystallises, refashions and incorporates living and soul-stirring imageries and visions for the learners. In fact, the role of every teacher educator almost entirely depends on how she/he is in a very sound position to foresee the canvas of inwardness painted not by bare instructions doled out in dull classrooms or elsewhere for her/his trainees but by the colour as it were of inwardness and vast expanse of the mind and the heart, empathy and sympathy well spread out in the grand panorama of teaching learning. In order to be on the right avenue of progress in her/his assignment, she/he ought to spontaneously and continuously prove the fact that she/he is an eternal learner.

Indeed, as a professional teacher educator, one cannot but pay attention to educate the teacher-trainees or would be teachers in consolidating and re-strengthening the foundation of teaching as a matter of enriched tradition. Side by side with this mission, she/he would also bear in mind that the rich tradition in teaching is a positive pointer to challenge which signals newer avenues of rebuilding the legacy of advancement in teaching learning. It is the adventurous teacher educator who instills in her/his teachers to undertake teaching as an adventure, a quest and a challenge 'to strive to seek to find and not to yield' in order to come out of the stagnant and dry shell of tradition that normally prompts imitation. In this connection, Professor Highet characteristically puts the following words of advice:

> If there has never been a good scientist at your school, you may want to be a physicist yourself, but you will not be apt to work so hard, and you will have more doubts and divagations.. if five or six Fellows of the Royal Society have been trained in the same laboratory, perhaps by the same masters, you will have clear targets to aim at. Even a failure will spur you on instead of discouraging you. They failed too. You must not fail again. Work. It is not necessary to model yourself on any individual. You can be yourself, unlike them all. You must equal them first, then excel them. Work. What they did, you can do, more.
>
> At this point tradition appeals to the same instinct as the master who sets four or five clever boys to the same job, knowing they will do far better in competition than working separately. Progress is successful rivalry with the past. As soon as reverence for tradition shrinks to nothing more than dutiful tradition, it becomes a deadening weight. As long as tradition provides an urge to strong, constant, and varied creative activity, it is a healthy stimulus and a wise guide.[3]

One of the greatest challenges for a teacher trainee and, for that end-in-view teacher educator is how to ask questions. Really, questioning is a science of all sciences and an art of all arts in the assignment of teaching and learning. Surprisingly, this important aspect of teaching is sometimes not given due importance in teacher education, thanks to routine-shy professionalism! That refinement in the presentation and application of appropriate and apposite questioning is the key to success in teaching and teacher education needs no explanation. Here is a fine and really very significant specimen which will always act as a stimulant to professional advancement:

> Never underestimate the power of a well-put question to illuminate the darkness. Students who have been passively absorbing information and allowing it to trickle out almost as fast as it was poured in will often come to life and take an active interest in their work when questions start flying. But the real value of the question-period at the end is for the conscientious students. It is worthwhile to read through a lecture-notebook kept by a student of good intelligence and industry. The gaps and misunderstandings in it will astound you. Often these youngsters are afraid to ask you to fill in the gaps, because they do not want to give themselves away. They think you will snub them, or answer perfunctorily. If you do, you are committing a crime. Instead, you should make it easy for them to ask for corrections, full names, the exact figures, the complete references. Don't simply wait for them to demand help. Offer it. You have not always spoken clearly. Foreign names and complex formulas are difficult to write down quickly. A cough will cover up half a vital sentence; and, in many cities nowadays, at least five minutes of every hour's teaching is made inaudible by the roar of transport aircraft apparently flying just above the roofs. The last few meetings of the class are your opportunity to wash away all that mud, and reveal your own lost pearls.[4]

The success of teacher education is to regain the lost paradise of 'lost pearls'. In professional development of teacher educators, reflective practice is crucial to teaching learning. It is a process of teaching that considers every learner teacher to be devoted to the practice of creative and critical thinking. As Harrison significantly asserts:

> Thinking about *reflective practice* as a concept is crucial since we do need to be clear about what it means. Whether we are beginning teachers, university education tutors or school

> mentors involved in school-based training, it is important that all of us have a chance to clarify what we understand by it and what we expect to entail. Our starting point is that it is much more than just *thinking about teaching*. It can be thought about in terms of asking searching questions about experience and conceptualised as both a state of mind and an ongoing type of behaviour.
>
> ** ** ** ** ** ** **
>
> Reflecting on aspects of teaching practice is usually fairly instinctive for most beginning teachers. You will focus mentally on particular problems or dilemmas that are to do with how a particular teaching session went. Often, perhaps with the aid of a lesson evaluation form, you will identify what went well during the teaching session, or to identify what could be tried out in other types of teaching sessions. This takes you from an essentially technical kind of reflection towards a more practical level, in which you begin to examine the interpretative assumptions you are making in your work.[5]

The role of the teacher educator is to inspire the teacher-trainees to cultivate self-awareness. It is really a very challenging job. The teacher educator cannot but ensure the fact that she/he acts like an explorer in chalking out the essential points of self-awareness for a new teacher, which contribute a lot to make every new teacher attentive and explicit in the development of self-awareness by means of involvement of either individual or group activity as situation demands or reflexive practice calls forth. As Harrison suggests:

(a) You are very new to the teaching profession.

After some very early experiences in the classroom, think about your answers to the questions below. Then share your thoughts with other beginning teachers after attempting to answer the following questions:

What kind of status does teaching have?

What does it mean to you, personally, to take on the mantle of 'teacher?

What public images are there of teachers with which you can identify?

How might new teachers begin to combine their personal and professional identities? (Accept that, for some, this might be experienced as the inability to be oneself).

What is your overall philosophy of teaching and learning?

What assumption (explicit or implicit) about the nature of students' learning are inherent in your approaches to teaching?

(b) Try to return to the final two questions in three and. Then, six months' time and answer them again.

What changes to your philosophy and your assumptions have taken place?

Specifically, have there been any changes to your general approach to teaching and learning, for example, in terms of you 'reaching out' to all the students in your classes?[6]

Professional development of teacher educators also needs a critical approach to teaching teacher-trainees with a foresight in regard to reviewing whatever teaching items are discussed, reacted, shared, evaluated and allowed to be enriched by the latter. It is also necessary that every teacher educator is precise, decisive and refined in the strategies for reflection through celebration of some of the best answers or strategies adopted by the learner teacher who has significantly inspired her/his learners to innovate and critically assess any item or component of teaching learning. Necessary inputs are to be cautiously provided to the latter so that the process of looking back is minimised as best as possible and the best of reflective and creative appreciation finds a spontaneous and unhindered outlet.

Decision-making in teaching for celebration of success is a pointer to how far a teacher foresees the success of effective teaching. For this, every teacher educator may keep a record of the assignments with which teacher-trainees are entrusted and the constraints negotiated or likely to be negotiated as and when necessary. A smart teacher educator introduces a festival of luminous teaching strategies for a wide range of teacher-trainees and relegates judiciously to the background so that freedom and joy in teaching learning are allowed to have natural manifestation. The five-fold avenue of select-describe-analyse-appraise-transform gets the right choice of efflorescence, and there is the key to desirable success in teacher education.

Classroom communication plays one of the most significant roles in effective teaching. Teacher education should ensure the fact that teacher educators are always conscious of training teachers in classroom communication from psycho-social points of view in particular. This will guarantee effectiveness in teaching learning and pupil motivation in creative and reflective thinking. Teachers then will be able to teach structured lessons by giving importance to pupil interest in activities and employ interactive teaching methods, collaborative group work and provide them with the opportunities of planning and managing their own teaching learning best suited to the interests and aptitudes of their learners. In this connection, Professor Pollard observes:

> Communicating is a complicated business and it is not surprising that it frequently goes wrong. In the rapidity of encoding and decoding processes, there are endless possibilities for misunderstanding. Of course, language skills are fundamental but, since communication involves people, it requires social skills as well. In addition, since communication is usually focussed on some meaningful topic, it calls for appropriate cognitive capacities-knowing something about the subject under consideration and being able to think about and process what we want to communicate to others and what they are trying to communicate to us. Nor can we forget the attitudes of the participants, the relationship between them, and the context itself, for these add another layer of meanings to encounter.
>
> Para-verbal and non-verbal features of oral language contribute to the effectiveness of how we communicate. Apart from what we say, a great deal is conveyed by how we say it. Thus, tone of voice, pace, pitch, volume and how we project our voice are all part of the communication process. In addition, there are non-verbal aspects such as looks and gestures, and the ways in which we move, which accompany what we say. These can

> sometimes extend our meanings but they can also sometimes confuse or even contradict what we say. This may be particularly true in communication between people from different cultures and backgrounds where different meanings may be ascribed to non-verbal features of talk. For example, looking directly at someone when speaking to them is acceptable behaviour in some cultures but considered the height of bad manners or a sign of disrespect to others.[7]

The quest for teacher education in keeping pace with the needs of the learners as individuals as one of the learner-centred approaches is a welcome strategy in which teacher trainees should be intensively involved. Care should be taken to see that teacher educators themselves exercise this individually and share their views and opinions with their student-trainees. What should act as a solid background for this type of exercise as teacher educators? What are probable or exact settings for exercise of individuality? Perhaps the following might act as a positive guideline:

> If we argue that individuals have learning needs, we are suggesting the necessity of an uncovering process to discover what these needs are. In many ways, this is manifested in the developing practices of guidance and counselling as a central component of learner-centred approaches. What this implies is that the needs are inherent in the person, that once we probe beyond the wants and desires we shall discover the learning needs which we can seek to meet. It is a stance that sees needs as embedded in individuals, the start of the learning process, rather than an outcome of previous learning and the very process of learning that takes place in the discovery of needs. It suggests a pathological view of the learner. We discover what is wrong with learners, what they need to learn to become better individuals, and then provide the relevant balms.

> In working with persons to discover learning needs, we are encouraging them to name certain of their experiences as needs, i.e., learning requirements which are fundamental to them-and then to give names to those needs. More importantly, we are encouraging them to view their needs as belonging to

> them as individuals, decontextualised from the social relations that frame their life possibilities. We are helping persons to construct identities for themselves—to name the unnamed—and this is not a neutral process. It is both part of and an aspect of the prior assumption of the individualism inscribed in learner-centred approaches.[8]

Teacher education for the purpose of professional development of teacher educators will have to overhaul its structures, initiatives and programmes of activities well-suited to the advancement of teaching learning. A humanistic and really vibrant teacher education cannot but address the diverse issues related to its programmes of activities. The recommendations of the Working Group for Teacher Education of the XI Plan as set forth below will not only signal a new direction for professional development of teacher educators but also ensure the education and teaching a synchroniser of all institutions in terms of true professionalism:

> Setting up of Schools of *Education* in selected (30) university departments including the RIEs for breaking the isolation of elementary and secondary teacher education from the mainstream and integrating it with higher education. The Schools will have Centres for pre-service teacher education, curriculum research policy and educational development, learning and pedagogic studies, assessment and evaluation, professional development of teacher educators and teacher education curricula and teacher resource and academic support.
>
> Setting up one *Inter-University Centre* at the national level functioning under the UGC to co-ordinate the Schools in terms of academic content: redesigning teacher education curricula, developing curriculum materials, commissioning of materials in regional languages, setting up of web portals on curriculum and pedagogic materials for teacher education. The mandate for Centre would be to provide an integrated focus on elementary and secondary levels of school education.
>
> Instituting *Specialised Centres of Education* in lead national level institutions like IISc, Homi Bhava Centre, TIFR to offer

sandwiched post-graduate courses of three years' duration (B.Ed. For two years or M.Ed. For three years) towards developing a specialised cadre of Senior Secondary school teachers and teacher educators.

Establishing four *Regional Centres of Educational Management* in the IIMs and NUEPA to provide a post-graduate degree in educational management for Heads of DIETs, SCERTs.

The *Centre for Professional Development of Teacher Educators* will offer Master's programme in elementary education/secondary education with specialisation in curriculum and pedagogic studies in mathematics/science/ social science education and assessment.

Reorientation of select secondary school teachers for elementary school teaching through Advance Diploma in elementary education; focussed programmes of professional development for DIET/SCERT faculty including curriculum and pedagogic studies and disciplinary knowledge base.

Special emphasis for professional renewal of existing teacher educators through Refresher Courses for all teacher educators including elementary school teachers in the proposed University Schools of Education and special subject refresher courses by university departments.

Institute teacher educator fellowships to undertake research with provision for mentoring about 200 or more fellowships for teacher educators working in government or aided institutions of teacher education. The fellowships will offer opportunities for attachment to institutions of higher learning to pursue teaching and research for a period of two years.

Periodic academic enrichment activities-public lectures, film and book discussion sessions, need-based issues, short-term orientation courses on teaching-learning skills, meta-learning strategies related to different curricular areas and child development, pedagogical aspects related to reading, writing, thinking and instructional design theories for curriculum developers.

The *Centre for Teacher Resource and Academic Support*: Provision of teacher resources, children's literature, variety of school curricula, textbooks, multi-media materials, internet access; platform for teacher interaction, faculty exchange, seminars, study sessions, academic support, face-to-face as well as through ICT; development of learning and teaching materials for use in schools and sharing across schools.[9]

Teacher educators in teacher education always look forward to translating the mission, vision, objectives and goals of teaching learning in perfection and poignancy. It is a challenge that welcomes immense possibilities and great promises yet to be responded and fulfilled.

Are the sponsors and receivers aware of the spirit of excellence even now eluding almost everywhere?

References

1. *National Curriculum Framework for Teacher Education: Towards Preparing Professional and Humane Teacher,* National Council for Teacher Education, New Delhi, 2009, pp. 76-77.
2. Sri Aurobindo: "Education of the Child", *Education and the Growing Child,* Sri Aurobindo Institute of Research in Social Sciences, Sri Aurobindo Society, Pondicherry, 1996, pp. 1-2.
3. Highet, Gilbert: *The Art of Teaching,* University Paperbacks, Methuen, London, 1963, p. 141.
4. *Ibid.,* pp. 148-149.
5. Dymoke, Sue and Harrison, Jennifer: "Professional Development and the Reflective Practitioner" by Jennifer Harrison, *Reflective Teaching and Learning,* Sage, South Asia Edition, 2010, p. 8.
6. *Ibid.,* pp. 16-17.
7. Pollard, Andrew: *Reflective Teaching and Learning,* Continuum, London, South Asia Edition, 2006, pp. 272-273.

8. Edwards, Richard: "Meeting Individual Learner Needs: Power, Subject, Subjection", *Knowledge, Power and Learning* (Ed. Carrie Paechter, Margaret Preedy, Daniel Scott and Janet Soler), Paul Chapman Publishing Limited, London, 2001, p. 41.
9. *National Curriculum Framework for Teacher Education: Towards Preparing Professional and Humane Teacher,* National Council for Teacher Education, New Delhi, 2009, pp. 84-86.

7 Teacher Education and the Individual Learner: Setting New Agenda for Negotiating Needs

Teacher education in the twenty-first century emphasises on the excellence of the individual learner as one of the most important assignments in education for fullness. It welcomes the diverse needs of the learner as significant transformers in the behaviour of each learner in the process of learning. Accordingly, the teacher and, for that end-in-view, teacher educator take every teaching strategy for orientation of learner behaviour in terms of what the latter approves or disapproves, likes or dislikes in the pursuit of learning. This three-fold advantage. First, the learner exercises ample freedom in exposing his/her learning interest and motivation, attitude and appreciation to the teacher either directly or indirectly as she/he considers appropriate. Second, the need-based planning of teaching as the teacher or/and teacher educator launches for the individual learner gets an opportunity to be redesigned in accordance with behavioural pattern of learning by the learner so much so that teaching-learning undergoes quality and excellence. Third, the individual learner needs finds sufficient care and advancement in the process of teaching learning as a positive and vibrant exercise of education for knowing, doing and being as the best outcome of teaching-learning activities.

At the outset, it must be admitted that it is impossible to accommodate all individual learner needs within a limited period of time that is under the control of teaching-learning in an educational institution at any stage of teaching-learning. Moreover, it also demands appropriate scanning of learner needs where the delegation of authority should be rationally and amicably settled. At the same time, the power to take decisions on the learner needs is not altogether a constraint but an optimistic possibility of advancement in reaching the truth in teaching-learning under a real life situation. As Foucault explicitly observes:

> Power and knowledge directly imply one another: that there is no power relation without the correlative constitution of a field of knowledge, nor any knowledge that does not presuppose and constitute at the same time power relation.[1]

Again,

> We must cease once and for all to describe the effects of power in negative terms: it 'excludes', it 'represses', it 'censors', it 'abstracts', it 'masks' it 'conceals'. In fact, power produces; it produces realities; it produces domains of objects and rituals of truth.[2]

Why do we emphasise on the identification, analysis, verification, application and evaluation of learner needs ? The reasons are not difficult to find out. In fact, what the individual learner needs transpire is the net result of what teaching stands for in the ultimate analysis. If the individual learner needs are justified in terms of the different and appropriate strategies of teaching that ensures right thinking, right understanding and right appreciating values and ethos in tune with activities and attainments suited to the welfare of the society for democratic living, one might say that the role of the teacher, and, for that purpose, the role of the teacher educator is justified to a great extent.

The essential components serving as the backdrop of negotiating individual learner needs may be identified as follows for better teaching:

(i) An error-free idea or concept that there is an intrinsic and fundamental worth of every individual learner's map of perfection,

(ii) The individual learner should be given to highlight and exercise on the choice she/he has made, subject to the fact that it more or less comes under the purview of reliability and validity in terms of teaching-learning,

(iii) The principal issues arising out of such choice have the viable tendency to consolidate the teaching-learning process from time to time in consonance with the learner needs,

(iv) The learner-centred approaches in tune with the needs already identified have all possible avenues of transfer and transcendence for the advancement of positive and reflective thinking of both the teacher and the learner at different stages of exposition,

(v) The learner becomes more responsive to learning needs as a stepping stone to crystallise some of the essential components of innovative thinking where the role of the teacher is to stimulate the learner in undertaking newer challenges by manipulating viable opportunities as and when available.

In case of the adult learner, the learning needs should be contextualised as the teacher considers apposite. Sometimes a few alternative items of interest may be introduced, where the teacher would be keen enough to assume the probable line of reaction of the learner in accommodating and enriching the outcome of the needs already chosen to be followed or translated into reality in learning. However, the theory and practice of individual learning should be intensified by the teacher who might undergo training to be guided and supervised at least by the concerned teacher educator. In this connection, the suggestion put forward by Professor Moore is very significant from the particular point of view of reflection:

> The theory and the practice of individual learning are founded on a set of values and assumptions which many of us will share, and which are vital to the health of our society. * * * They include a belief in the intrinsic and fundamental worth of every individual soul. They include the liberal view that the individual should be free to exercise choice, and to grow in an individual way, unimpeded by state control and direction * * * But individual learning is a mode of education which reflects, and also promotes, the very values which give our society its meaning, for ultimately it is the well-being and growth of each individual which is the purpose of, and justification for, the democratic state.[3]

For an enlivening and refreshing climate of negotiating learner needs, it is time to rethink and introduce revitalised programmes of stimulating and thrilling programmes on innovations in teaching. Indeed, every teacher should be encouraged in innovative teaching which has its far reaching and illuminating effects on sensitising and refining learner needs in terms of a vibrant curriculum. As the NCF categorically emphasises:

> Individual teachers often explore new ways of transacting the curriculum in addressing the needs of students within their specific classroom context (including constraints of space, large numbers, absence of teaching aids, diversity in the student body, the compulsions of examinations, and so on). These efforts, often pragmatic but also creative and ingenious, by and large remain invisible to the school and the larger teaching community, and are usually not valued by teachers themselves. The sharing of teaching experiences and diverse classroom practices can provide opportunities for an academic discourse to develop within schools as teachers interact with and learn from each other. This will also encourage new ideas and facilitate innovation and experimentation. How can innovative and creative ways of teaching and learning be encouraged and supported by the system so that they can become a body of practice that can be brought to a stage when they can be built back into the system? For a start, there is a need to create structured spaces within schools, and at the level of the cluster and block where teachers are encouraged to share and discuss classroom practices and experiences. If seen as worthwhile, some of these ideas and practices can be systematically followed up. It is also important to bring together groups of teachers within and across schools and provide support to them in terms of resources as well as time to work together. There is also a need for documentation and research of identified 'good practices'.[4]

In view of the above, teacher education must ensure a wide canvas of negotiating learner needs where teaching-learning cannot but be innovative, critical and reflective. Designing in-service programmes for teachers in order to be justified to negotiating the diverse needs of every learner who really craves for necessary guidance and supervision in her/his strategies of learning at the different levels of difficulties is now-a-days becoming obligatory. The following principles as suggested by the National Curriculum Framework for Teacher Education (NCFTE) deserve sincere attention and implementation:

> Programmes must build on the principle of creating 'spaces' for sharing of experiences of communities of teachers among themselves, to build stronger shared professional basis of individual experiences and ideas. Giving teachers a space to develop and hear their own voices is of utmost importance.
>
> Programmes must be designed with a clear sense of their aims and how the strategies of the programme are going to achieve these aims. This alone can ensure that programmes remain on track and 'alive' rather than routine when they are implemented. This may also require then, that every group of trainers either directly participate in the design of the programme, keeping in mind a specific group of teachers, or adapts a given programme to a specific group of teachers. Programmes also need to include a plan for post-programme support and include training/orientation of support faculty of the same.
>
> All programmes must find acceptance of their aims with the teachers' group concerned, regarding whether they need such a programme and why they are to attend it. The principle of choice of programmes to attend, based on some valid assessment of professional requirement, would provide a sound basis for in-service programmes, especially those that are of a long duration and which seek to impact practice. One size cannot fit all.
>
> Interactivity must not be compromised on any account. Large numbers and the use of electronic media in the place of human interaction compromise on the non-negotiable.
>
> The content of programmes must be such that teachers can relate to it from their own experience and also find opportunities to reflect on these experiences.

> The approach of motivating for change must not put the burden on individual development alone, but must also recognise and respond to the structural issues that affect teacher's day-to-day practice. Equally, structures and people in supervisory positions must be educated to support and provide space to encourage teachers to plan and practice autonomously.
>
> Programmes that seek to develop or alter basic practice need to be planned towards extensive interactions over time with the same resource group.[5]

Keeping in view the above perspective in teacher education, the needs of the learners at every stage demand a thorough study in terms of multi-dimensional contribution to the development of personality. The teacher is never isolated from any need whatsoever or however of the learner, whenever there is a call for awareness in teaching-learning, the learner and the teacher enjoy the real warmth of the quest for knowledge and experience as the fountain of freedom and joy in a conjoint and mutually communicated climate of erudition and culture, edification and intrinsic exercise. The needs, then, turn out to be the oysters of fullness in the advancement of excellence and quality assurance.

A new dawn of awareness to dynamic and vibrant teacher education in the twenty-first century promises education of a very high quality and excellence by incorporating newer agenda for teacher enrichment professionally. The aesthetics of teaching has set forth new horizons of teaching for the exercise of sensitising finer components of humane culture and civilisation, ethos and moorings, heritage and tradition. The concept of de-schooling in relation to teaching-learning is gaining newer grounds in the efflorescence of altruistic personality development. Already, teaching and teacher education are on the tip-toe of newer avenues of studies and researches on how the needs of every learner can be processed under a multiple scanner for quality and excellence. The teacher, however, is never lost in the eventuality of all these newer avenues being consolidated and synchronised from time to time. Her/ His catholicity of vision in teaching as her/his own, typically and characteristically her/his very own will ever remain illuminating like a pole star. Here is a classic example:

> A display of good creative memory by a teacher helps the young in one of their most difficult jobs. Their attention is lively and their perception is keen, but they find it very hard to connect things. Many of the facts they learn merely drop into their minds like blocks of metal, and lie there. At examinations they take out the blocks, polish them, and show them to us. Then they put them back, or sometimes throw them away. If the facts simply remain on deposit, however neatly packed and highly polished, their possessors are not educated. The business of the teacher is to pass currents of interest and energy through the facts, while they are being learnt and afterwards, so that they melt, fuse, become interconnected, acquire life, and grow into vital parts of the minds which hold them. One excellent way to do this is to demonstrate how apparently remote facts are originally linked, and that can sometimes be done more happily as improvisation than as a prepared part of a lesson. When it comes off, the teacher's reward is there: he sees face after face light up as two blank areas of the brain, with the connections flashing between them, come alive.[6]

The art of drawing out what is already within the learner's mind is a challenge for the teacher. The challenge must be accepted; otherwise, it is futile on the part of the teacher even to have a glimpse of, and being justified to, the learner's potentiality. As soon as the learner does justice to his potentiality, the teacher receives her/his reward surely but silently without exposing her/his personality.

Negotiating the diverse needs of the learner by the teacher either inside or outside the classroom is a never ending challenge, and, as it is so, so is the profession of teaching alluring and assuring. The learner's needs are the seeds of teaching that await germination under absolute care and caution, nursing and appreciation. Here the scale of success is dependent on how the needs are considered to be the most essential components of the learner in the persistent process of learning. No need is inconsistent or irrelevant, undesirable and redundant. It all depends on how the learner is prompted towards identifying, analysing and evaluating every need in terms of her/his interest and skill, aptitude and attitude and how is related to arouse curiosity and logical reasoning, askance and appreciation. Moreover, the points of usability and comparability, in-depth vision and elucidation are also associated with it. Naturally, it takes into account the advantage or disadvantage of the decisive role of the learner whose perception, intrinsic as well as extrinsic is very closely associated. As a matter of fact, no need gets lost unless evaluated, and this becomes very crucial at a stage of learning when the learner is a child, young and adolescent one.

When would we be sincerely and heartily justified to the needs of every individual learner in education?

References

1. Foucault, M.: *Discipline and Punish,* Hammondsworth, Peregrine Books, 1977, p. 27.
2. *Ibid.,* p. 174.
3. Moore, M.: "The Individual and Adult Learner" in M. Tight (ed), *Adult Learning and Education,* Croom Helm, 1983, pp. 153/169.
4. *National Curriculum Framework 2005,* National Council of Educational Research and Training, New Delhi, 2005, p. 120.
5. *National Curriculum Framework for Teacher Education—Towards Preparing Professional and Humane Teacher,* National Council for Teacher Education, New Delhi, 2009, p. 66.
6. Highet Gilbert: *The Art of Teaching,* Methuen, London, 1963, p. 58.

8 Vibrant Teacher Education: Vivekananda's Viewpoints

A pioneer in education for all time and all places for one and all, Swami Vivekananda's philosophy of education and teacher preparation is very significant for excellence and ascent of man. As a firm believer in the education of the self by the self and for the self, he draws our attention to the role of the teacher as a sincere and devoted task master in enabling the learner to justify his/her perfection already in him/her as best as possible. He gives importance to teaching as a living and dynamic symbol of exercise of the boundless possibilities of humans to attain the power to unfold and manifest inherent fullness in all directions with utmost endeavour for perfection.

Moderation and modification are the two essential components of meaningful and purposeful teaching. In teacher education, these two components serve as hallmarks of quality and excellence. Vivekananda explicitly explains this point:

> Time is merely the measures of our thoughts, and the thought being inconceivably swift, there is no limit to the speed with which we can live the life ahead. So it cannot be stated how long it would take to live all future life. It might be in a second, or it might take fifty lifetimes. It depends on the intensity of the desire. The teaching must therefore be modified according to

> the needs of the taught. The consuming fire is already for all, even water and chunks of ice quickly consume. Fire a mass of birdshot, one at least will strike; give a man a whole museum of truths, he will at once take what is suited to him. Past life has moulded our tendencies; give to the taught in accordance with his tendency. Intellectual, mystical, devotional, practical-make one the basis, but teach the others with it. Intellect must be balanced with love, the mystical nature with reason, while practice must form part of every method. Take every one where he stands and push him forward. Religious teaching must always be constructive, not destructive.
>
> Each tendency shows the life-work of the past, the line or radius along which that man must move. All radii lead to the centre. Never even attempt to disturb anyone's tendencies; to do that puts back both teacher and taught. When you teach *Jnana,* you must become a *Jnani* and stand mentally exactly where the taught stands. Similarly in every other *Yoga*. Develop every faculty as if it were the only one possessed, this is the true secret of harmonious development. That is, get extensity with intensity, but not at its expense. We are infinite. There is no limitation in us, we can be as intense as the most devoted Mohammedan and as broad as the most roaring atheist.[1]

That a teacher is essentially a learner first and thereafter attempts to teach as best as possible by means of utilising the dividends of learning is the primary principle of teaching. How does he/she learn and from whom? How to be the most inspiring teacher? As answers to all these questions and similar other one's, Vivekananda's invaluable words serve as eternal guidelines:

> There are many who, though immersed in ignorance, yet, in the pride of their hearts, fancy they know everything, and not only do not stop there, but offer to take others on their shoulders; and thus the blind leading the blind, falls into the ditch. * * * "Fools dwelling in darkness, wise in their own conceit, and puffed up with vain knowledge, go round and round staggering to and fro, like blind men led by the blind."—

> (Katha Up., I. II. 5), the world is full of these. Every one wants to be a teacher, every beggar wants to make a gift of a million dollars! Just as these beggars are ridiculous, so are these teachers.[2]

Teaching is a reciprocal activity. It is a conjoint and communicated endeavour in the pursuit of knowledge and erudition, appreciation and edification. Vivekananda reminds us of the fact that the true teacher always strives for the best ways to ignite the best thought to be exercised and appreciated in the best manner. Here the distinction between the teacher and the taught merges in the conjugal quest for teaching and learning for fullness.

Vibrant teacher education should always be in the perfect fusion between the teacher and the taught. This fusion necessitates the eligibility of the teacher in imparting the right direction to the taught by illumining the lamp of curiosity and right thinking at the right moment towards the right direction for manifestation. At the same time, the learner must prove his/her openness as a receiver of whatever his/her teacher teaches.

Recalling his intense and respectful relationship with his Master as a teacher unparalleled and incomparable, Vivekananda adroitly describes the role of the ideal teacher:

> Few understand the power of thought. If a man goes into a cave, shuts himself in, and thinks one really great thought and dies, that thought will penetrate the walls of that cave, vibrate through space, and at last penetrate the whole human race. Such is the power of thought; be in no hurry therefore to give your thoughts to others. First have something to give. He alone teaches who has something to give, for teaching is not talking, teaching is not imparting doctrines, it is communicating. Spirituality can be communicated just as really as I can give you a flower. This is true in the most literal sense. This idea is very old in India and finds illustration in the West in the theory, in the belief, of apostolic succession. Therefore first make character—that is the highest duty you can perform. Know Truth for yourself, and there will be many to whom you can teach it afterwards; they will all come. This was the attitude of

> my Master. He criticised no one. For years I lived with that man, but never did I hear those lips utter one word of condemnation for any sect. He had the same sympathy for all sects; he had found the harmony between them. A man may be intellectual, or devotional, or mystic, or active; the various religions represent one or the other of these types. Yet it is possible to combine all the four in one man, and this is what future humanity is going to do. That was his idea. He condemned no one, but saw the good in all.
>
> People came by thousands to see and hear this wonderful man who spoke in a patois every word of which was forceful and instinct with light. For it is not what is spoken, much less the language in which it is spoken, but it is the personality of the speaker which dwells in everything he says that carries weight. Every one of us feels this at times. We hear most splendid orations, most wonderfully reasoned-out discourses, and we go home and forget them all. At other times we hear a few words in the simplest language, and they enter into our lives, become part and parcel of ourselves and produce lasting results. The words of a man who can put his personality into them take effect, but he must have tremendous personality. All teaching implies giving and taking, the teacher gives and the taught receives, but the one must have something to give, and the other must be open to receive.[3]

The essential truth that a teacher does not teach but assists, inspires and stimulates the learners in the process of enrichment of self-thinking, self-reasoning and self-activity by means of introspection and self-evaluation should always be the guideline of teaching for enhancing quality and excellence. Education for understanding and appreciating self-respect and self-dependence can never wait. Vivekananda emphasises on that teaching where the role of the teacher is to teach in such a way where the learners are inspired by the lessons of self-development and self-control through self-activity and self-criticism for the onward march for negotiating greater challenges of life and society. He has hailed the decision of Lord Curzon, the-then Viceroy of India under the British rule, to abolish higher education because it was meant not for all but for the limited few in our country, and stressed on the teaching on how to be self-reliant through learning to do for a genuine learning to be as an incomparable process of education for advancement. As he strongly advocates:

> The teacher spoils everything by thinking that he is teaching. Thus Vedanta says that within man is all knowledge—even in a boy it is so—and it requires only an awakening, and that much is the work of a teacher. We have to do only so much for the boys that they may learn to apply their own intellect to the proper use of their hands, legs, ears, eyes, etc., and finally everything will become easy. But the root is religion. Religion is as the rice, and everything else, like the curries. Taking only curries causes indigestion, and so is the case of taking rice alone. Our pedagogues are making parrots of our boys and ruining their brains by cramming a lot of subjects into them. Looking from one standpoint, you should rather be grateful to the Viceroy for his proposal of reforming the university system, which means practically abolishing higher education; the country will, at least, feel some relief by having breathing time. Goodness gracious! What a fuss and fury about graduating, and after a few days all cool down! And after all that, what is it they learn but that what religion and customs we have are all bad, and what the Westerners have are all good! At last, they cannot keep the wolf from the door! What does this matter if this higher education remains or goes? It would be better if the people got a little technical education, so that they might find work and earn their bread, instead of dawdling about and crying for service.[4]

Teaching for cultivation of values is yet to be given appropriate emphasis in teacher education. The plans and programmes in teaching for the exercise of finer sensibilities like humility, tolerance, kindness, magnanimity, etc., are few and far between even at the formative stages of education where teachers lack sufficient and careful training in the teaching of values. In teacher education for advancement of the inner-spirit of values, every teacher should act like a mirror to the learner as an "eye-opener". As regards teaching lessons on religion for cultivation of values, Vivekananda significantly points out:

> The "books in the running brooks, sermons in stones, and good in every thing" is all very true as a poetical figure; but nothing can impart to a man a single grain of truth unless he has the undeveloped germs of it in himself. To whom do the stones and brooks preach sermons? To the human soul, the lotus of whose inner holy shrine is already quick with life. And the light which causes the beautiful opening out of this lotus comes always from the good and wise teacher. When the heart has thus been opened, it becomes fit to receive teaching from the stones or the brooks, the stars, or the sun, or the moon, or from any thing which has its existence in our divine universe; but the unopened heart will see in them nothing but mere stones or mere brooks. A blind man may go to a museum, but he will not profit by it in any way; his eyes must be opened first, and then alone he will be able to learn what the things in the museum can teach.[5]

Vibrant teacher education must prioritise active and inspiring involvement of the student-teacher who must be aware of teaching for self-activity and self-development. This necessitates a close bond of relationship between the teacher and the taught. In teacher education programmes on teaching should be backed by a new framework of the curriculum where this bond of kindred relationship is sincerely and affectionately maintained. Vivekananda significantly reminds us about the importance of cultivating this endearing, homely and living relationship between the teacher and the taught:

> The teacher is not a man who comes just to teach me, and I pay him so much, and there it ends. In India it is really like an adoption. The teacher is more than my own father, and I am truly his child, his son in every respect. I owe him obedience and reverence first, before my own father even; because, they say, the father gave me this body, but he showed me the way to salvation, he is greater than father. And we carry this love, this respect for our teacher all our lives. * * * I adopt my disciples.

> Sometimes the teacher will be a young man and the disciple a very old man. But never mind, he is the son, and he calls me "Father", and I have to address him as my son, my daughter, and so on.[6]

The bond of living relationship between the teacher and the taught as Vivekananda describes above ought to be regenerated in our present system of education. This will definitely bring about a radical change in the climate of teaching-learning that always welcomes the cultivation and dissemination of *shraddha* (respect) in the total system of education in general and teacher education in particular.

Elsewhere, Vivekananda also emphasises on the same spirit of mutual respect and faith very explicitly in terms of his own vision of teacher education. According to him, the teacher is more than parents for freedom of the soul that is blessed with the efflorescence of rebirth:

> The disciple must have faith in the Guru (teacher). In the West the teacher simply gives intellectual knowledge; that is all. The relationship with the teacher is the greatest in life. My dearest and nearest relative in life is my Guru; next, my mother; then my father. My first reverence is to the Guru. If my father says, "Do this", and my Guru says, "Do not do this", I do not do it. The Guru frees my soul. The father and mother give me this body; but the Guru gives me rebirth in the soul.[8]

Teacher education in the twenty-first century for training and development of spirituality is, let us frankly admit, at a very low ebb. That a genuine teacher is not in the body in terms of imparting lessons on spirituality but in the mind is appallingly absent from our present day curriculum framework in teacher education. The current of vibrant spiritual education even in a country like ours has more or less been allowed to be almost extinct because neither teacher educators nor teacher-trainees are devoted to the education of spirituality as a stepping stone to the advancement of the learners for excellence and ascent in every direction. The education of the heart still pines for the fullness of the mind and the soul. The role of the teacher as a true transmitter of spirituality as Vivekananda reminds us needs re-thinking and re-translating into reality by means of a careful overhaul of teacher education:

> There is no reason why each of you cannot be a vehicle of the mighty current of spirituality.
>
> But first you must find a teacher, a true teacher, and you must remember that he is not just a man. You may get a teacher in the body; but a real teacher is not in the body; he is not the physical man—he is not as he appears to your eyes. It may be the teacher will come to you as a human being, and you will receive the power from him. Sometimes he will come in a dream and transmit things to the world. The power of the teacher may come to us in many ways. But for us ordinary mortals the teacher must come, and our preparation must go on till he comes.[8]

We attend lectures and read books, argue and reason about God and soul, religion and salvation. These are not spirituality, because spirituality does not exist in books or in theories or in philosophies. It is not in learning or reasoning, but in actual inner growth. Even parrots can learn things by heart and repeat them. If you become learned, what of it? Asses can carry whole libraries. So when real light will come, there will be no more of this learning from books—no book-learning. The man who cannot write even his own name can be perfectly religious, and the man with all the libraries of the world in his head may fail to be. Learning is not a condition of spiritual growth; scholarship is not a condition. The touch of the Guru, the transmittal of spiritual energy, will quicken your heart. Then will begin the growth. That is the real baptism by fire. No more stopping.

True teaching actives both self-teaching through self-learning. The role of the teacher is to allow the learner ample freedom to learn by herself/ himself. She/ He should never thrust anything because it goes against the learner's constitutional development and betrays self-learning. A true learner is always a teacher by herself/himself. Right from education of children at the early stage, our teachers should be oriented through education and training by adopting the principle of freedom to think and freedom to act in order to enjoy freedom to be as one ought to be with boundless possibilities of manifestation of inherent perfection. Vivekananda strongly advocates this in the teaching in general and the teaching of religion in particular as follows:

You cannot make a plant grow in soil unsuited to it. A child teaches itself. But you can help it to go forward in its own way. What you can do is not of the positive nature, but of the negative. You can take away the obstacles, but knowledge comes out of its own nature. Loosen the soil a little, so that it may come out easily. Put a hedge round it; see that it is not killed by anything, and there your work stops. You cannot do anything else. The rest is a manifestation from within its own nature. So with the education of a child; a child educates itself. You come to hear me, and when you go home, compare what you have learnt, and you will find you have thought out the same thing; I have only given it expression. I can never teach you anything: you will have to teach yourself, but I can help you perhaps in giving expression to that thought.

So in religion—more so—I must teach myself religion. What right has my father to put all sorts of nonsense into my head? Perhaps they are good, but they may not be my way. Think of the appalling that is in the world today, of the millions and millions of innocent children perverted by wrong ways of teaching. How many beautiful things which would have become wonderful spiritual truths have been nipped in the bud by this horrible idea of a family religion, a social religion, a national religion, and so forth. Think of what a mass of superstition is in your head just now about your childhood's religion, or your country's religion, and what an amount of evil it does, or can do. Man does not know what a potent power lies behind each thought and action. The old saying is true that, "Fools rush in where angels fear to tread," this should be kept in view from the very first. How? By this belief in *Ishta*. There are so many ideals; I have no right to say what shall be your ideal, to force any ideal in you. My duty should be to lay before you all the ideals I know of and enable you to see by your own constitution what you like best, and which is most fitted to you. Take up that one which suits you best and persevere in it. This is your *Ishta*, your special ideal.[9]

Admittedly, the teaching of spirituality as Vivekananda describes as above still remains outside the purview of teacher education. The advancement of education for identifying, exploring, analysing and evaluating education for inward depth of vision, and, for that end-in-view, expanding and enriching teacher education is yet to be cultivated by means of introducing dynamic and spirited programmes of training in teaching where a harmonious blending of challenging and stimulating theories and experiments serves as a pointer to education and teaching for the development of character and personality. The more a teacher is involved in the teaching of building a sound basis of development of personality through the exercise in character formation, the more are the possibilities for both the teacher and the learner to be justified to teaching and learning respectively. In fact, a time will come, and come it must when the teacher and the learner will be in perfect fusion in education for oneness of fullness in character and development of personality.

Vivekananda's primary concern for the role of the teacher is to create a suitable, appropriate and ideal environment of teaching-learning where the teacher proves herself/himself as an eternal and painstaking, vibrant and tolerant learner. Her/His continuous and sincere involvement in teaching should first be positively guaranteed by a strong urge to learn the learner. The components of learning the learner should obviously include the latter's attitude and aptitude to learning well and sufficiently supported by understanding and knowledge, interest and skill, motivation and will-force, temperament and appreciation. In the proper delineations and exposures of all these components, the teacher ought to prove her/his worth as an expert in introducing different strategies, for which the teacher educators concerned would inspire her/him to be more justified to the diverse world of every learner. No doubt, it is a really very challenging and difficult task; but who else than the teacher be the real partner or friend of the learner in quest of joy in learning for fullness?

Teacher education must give priority to training of the mind of each and every learner. For this, the teacher, as Vivekananda inspires, should be trained in directing the learner how to concentrate, think, work for true learning through continuous verification and evaluation, and finally, detach herself from the fruit of learning. Thus extinction of personality becomes the ultimate goal of teaching and learning where the teacher and the learner come under the same platform of education for ceaseless endeavour and achievement well-guided by self-reverence and self-modesty as the most distinctive traits for development of personality. As Swami Prabhananda poignantly asserts:

> Vivekananda concurred with contemporary thinkers when he asserted that the mind—the chief instrument of learning—deserves more attention than it had earlier conceived. Training the mind should be the student's highest priority, and not simply the accumulation, the memorising and the repeating of facts. In the long run, stuffing one's mind with information, technical skills and useless trivia only creates more problems if one's mind is not nourished and strengthened and made healthy. Yet training of the mind in all its aspects is conspicuously absent in today's education.
>
> ** ** ** ** ** ** **
>
> In doing anything—such as thinking, working with the hands, etc.,— the better the power of concentration the better the outcome will be. And this power of keeping the mind on the task can be improved. Training the mind to concentrate on a specific subject has several stages, the primary one being learning how to collect the mind and preventing it from running hither and thither. The student trains his mind to be more attentive and more 'mindful.'
>
> Next, the student must learn how to detach his mind from distractions that impose themselves in spite of himself. Then, simultaneously, he must direct the mind to the desired subject and focus the full force of his mind on it. To give an example, a convex lens gathers sunlight and focusses it on one point to burn a piece of paper. Likewise, when a mind becomes concentrated, it acquires tremendous power and is able to unlock the mysteries of the subject it is focussed upon.[10]

Teacher education for training of teacher students and freshers in humanistic and aesthetic education needs clearly spelt out mission, vision, objectives and endeavour. Right now, preparing enlightened and humane teacher has been given topmost priority in this direction. In fact, the role of the teacher is best evaluated in terms of her/his involvement in discharging humanistic and aesthetic duties and responsibilities to the best of her/his abilities. As such, in exercising the humanistic and aesthetic spirit in teaching-learning, some major issues like how to cultivate truth, beauty and goodness as invaluable lessons of development of altruistic personality, her/his positive approach to education for oneness of man is obligatory.

As a great visionary and harmoniser of humanism and aesthetics, Vivekananda welcomes a radical approach to religious ideals for teaching and learning of universal goodness. As a matter of fact, our trends in teacher education in this second decade of the twenty-first century look forward to overhauling the social viewpoints of education and teaching in understanding, appreciating and disseminating the right spirit of living and enlightened religion. As Vivekananda strongly asserts:

> Even at the present time we find many sects and societies, with almost the same ideas, fighting each other because one does not want to set forth those ideas in precisely the same way as another. Therefore, religions will have to broaden. Religious ideas will have to become universal, vast, and infinite; and then alone we shall have the fullest play of religion, for the power of religion has only just begun to manifest in the world. It is sometimes said that religions are dying out, that spiritual ideas are dying out of the world. To me it seems that they have just begun to grow. The power of religion, broadened and purified, is going to penetrate every part of human life so long as religion was in the hands of a chosen few or of a body of priests, it was in temples, churches, books, dogmas, ceremonials, forms, and rituals. But when we come to the real, spiritual, and universal concept, then, and then alone, religion will become real and living; it will come into our very nature, live in our every movement, penetrate every pore of our society, and be infinitely more a power for good than it has ever been before.
>
> What is needed is a fellow-feeling between the different types of religion, seeing that they all stand or fall together, a fellow-feeling which springs from mutual esteem and mutual respect,

> and not the condescending, patronising, niggardly expression of goodwill, unfortunately in vogue at the present time with many. And above all, this is needed between types of religious expression coming from the study of mental phenomena—unfortunately, even now laying exclusive claim to the name of religion—and those expressions of religion whose heads, as it were, are penetrating more into the secrets of heaven though their feet are clinging to earth, I mean, the so-called materialistic sciences.
>
> To bring about this harmony, both will have to make concessions, sometimes very large, nay more, sometimes painful, but each will find itself the better for the sacrifice and more advanced in truth. And in the end, the knowledge which is confined within the domain of time and space will meet and become one with that which is beyond them both, where the mind and senses cannot reach— the Absolute, the Infinite, the One without a second.[11]

To know the truth and, accordingly, disseminate it appropriately is the task of the teacher. In teacher education, the training of student-teachers and freshers greatly depends on how to introduce diverse programmes of activities closely related to the well-being of others. The role of the individual learner is unique. How to maintain and flourish this spirit of individuality is a great challenge for every teacher and, for that end-in-view, teacher educator. As a humanistic and spiritual connoisseur of teacher education, Vivekananda's altruistic and practical advice as follows will definitely serve as the guiding principle in bringing about a desirable and meaningful change in teacher education:

> It is a mistake to say "you and I "; say "I". It is I who am eating in millions of mouths; how can I be hungry? It is I who am working through an infinite number of hands; how can I be inactive? It is I who am living the life of the whole universe; where is death for me? I am beyond all life, beyond all death. Where shall I seek for freedom? I am free by my nature. Who can bind me— the God of this universe? The scriptures of the world are but little maps, wanting to delineate my glory, who am

> the only existence of the universe. Then what are these books to me? Thus says the Advaitist.
>
> "Know the truth and be free in a moment," all the darkness will then vanish. When man has seen himself as one with the Infinite Being of the universe, when all separateness has ceased, when all men and women, all gods and angels, all animals and plants, and the whole universe have melted into that Oneness, then all fear disappears. Can I hurt myself? Can I kill myself? Can I injure myself? Whom to fear? Can you fear yourself? Then will all sorrow disappear. What can cause me sorrow? I am the One Existence of the universe. Then all jealousies will disappear; of whom to be jealous? Of myself? Then all bad feelings disappear. Against whom can I have bad feeling? Against myself? There is none in the universe but I. And this is the one way, says the Vedantist, to knowledge. Kill out this differentiation, kill out this superstition that there are many.[12]

To select and organise the altruistic content for the curriculum in terms of the above is one of the fundamental ends-in-view of teacher education. Vivekananda points out the fact that it is the teacher, and the teacher alone, who has the infinite capacity for adjusting herself/himself and the learner to undertake newer adventures in education for quality and excellence, ascent and brilliance, transparency and transcendence. It is she/he, and she/he alone, who acts like a spark plug in creative, critical and reflective thinking of the learners, it is she/he, and she/he alone, who presents every concept of learning to the learners not merely as a compulsory and obligatory matter to be learnt as such but to analyse, compare, contrast, verify and, if necessary, recast and challenge in a positive pattern of thinking so long untouched or undiscovered in the arena of advancement or efflorescence for perfection. In the poignant words of Vivekananda:

> Do not try to disturb the faith of any man. If you can, give him something better; if you can, get hold of a man where he stands and give him a push upwards; do so, but do not destroy what he has. The only true teacher is he who can convert himself, as

> it were, into a thousand persons at a moment's notice. The only true teacher is he who can immediately come down to the level of the student, and transfer his soul to the student's soul and see through the student's eyes and hear through his ears and understand through his mind. Such a teacher can really teach and none else. All these negative, breaking-down, destructive teachers that are in the world can never do any good.[13]

As an incomparable inspirer of teacher education for understanding and appreciating the reality of truth as one fundamental concepts of religion in terms of spiritual fullness, he pays his homage to his great Saint Shri Ramakrishna Paramahamsa, who taught till the last breath 'repeating the most sacred word of the Veda', by reminding the eternal message:

> "Do not care for doctrines, do not care for dogmas, or sects, or churches, or temples; they count for little compared with the essence of existence for each man, which is spirituality; and the more this is developed in a man, the more powerful is he for good. Earn that first, acquire that, and criticise no one, for all doctrines and creeds have some good in them. Show by your lives that religion does not mean words, or names, or sects, but that it means spiritual realisation. Only those can understand who have felt. Only those who have attained to spirituality can communicate it to others, can be great teachers of mankind. They alone are the powers of light."
>
> The more such men are produced in a country, the more that country will be raised; and that country where such men absolutely do not exist is simply doomed, nothing can save it. Therefore, my Master's message to mankind is: "Be spiritual and realise truth for yourself," he would have you give up for the sake of your fellow-beings. He would have you cease talking about love for your brother, and set to work to prove your words. The time has come for renunciation, for realisation; and then you will see the harmony in all the religions of the world. You will know that there is no need of any quarrel. And then only you will be ready to help humanity. To proclaim and make clear the fundamental unity underlying all religions was

> the mission of my Master. Other teachers have taught special religions which bear their names, but this great teacher of the nineteenth century made no claim for himself. He left every religion undisturbed because he had realised that in reality they are all part and parcel of the one eternal religion."[14]

As an ardent follower of the great teacher, Vivekananda has serenely widened the vision of positive education of the child in understanding and translating the human spirit into vibrant contemplation and action. In this connection, one might recall one of the most characteristic and living suggestions on how to teach children; in "Indian Religious Thought", a lecture delivered in Brooklin, USA, he poignantly upholds:

> We should cultivate the optimistic temperament, and endeavour to see the good that dwells in everything. If we sit down and lament over the imperfection of our bodies and minds, we profit nothing; it is the heroic endeavour to subdue adverse circumstances that carries our spirit upwards. The object of life is to learn the laws of spiritual progress. Christians can learn from Hindus, and Hindus can learn from Christians. Each has made a contribution of value to the wisdom of the world.
>
> Impress upon your children that true religion is positive and not negative, that it does not consist in merely refraining from evil, but in a persistent performance of noble deeds. True religion comes not from the teaching of men or the reading of books; it is the awakening of the spirit within us, consequent upon pure and heroic action. Every child born into the world brings with it a certain accumulated experience from previous incarnations; and the impress of this experience is seen in the structure of its mind and body. The soul that reigns within is independent and creates the desire for freedom. If we are not free, how can we hope to make the world better? We hope that human progress is the result of the action of the human spirit. What the world is, and what we ourselves are, are the fruits of the freedom of the spirit.[15]

When would we follow the footprints of Swami Vivekananda and his great Master, Shri Ramakrishna Paramahamsa to glorify teacher education as the beacon light, as it were, of man and society for fullness and excellence?

References

1. Swami Vivekananda: *The Complete Works of Swami Vivekananda,* Advaita Ashrama, Kolkata, Mayavati Memorial Edition, 1989, Vol. VII, pp. 97-98.
2. *Ibid.,* Vol. III, p. 47.
3. *Ibid.,* Vol. IV, pp. 177-178.
4. *Ibid.,* Vol. V, pp. 366-367.
5. *Ibid.,* Vol. III, pp. 51-52.
6. *Ibid.,* Vol. VIII, p. 78.
7. *Ibid.,* p. 112.
8. *Ibid.,* pp. 113-114.
9. *Ibid.,* Vol. IV, pp. 55-56.
10. Swami Prabhananda: "Swami Vivekananda The Educationist Par Excellence", *Swami Vivekananda: My Idea of Education,* Advaita Ashrama, Kolkata, 2008, pp. 22-23.
11. Swami Vivekananda: *The Complete Works of Swami Vivekananda,* Advaita Ashrama, Kolkata, Mayavati Memorial Edition, 1989, Vol. II, pp. 68-69.
12. *Ibid.,* pp. 249-250.
13. *Ibid.,* Vol. IV, p. 183.
14. *Ibid.,* Vol. IV, p. 187.
15. *Ibid.,* p. 190.

9 Teacher Education and the Evolving Teacher: Sri Aurobindo's Guidelines

An unparalleled radical thinker in education and the role of the teacher, Sri Aurobindo considers education a self-evolving process where the teacher is merely a suggester and never an authoritarian or dictator in the process of discharging her/his duties and responsibilities. Education is a matter of self-inquiry by means of self-askance and self-criticism through self-analysis and self-evaluation. Therefore, freedom and joy in the process of learning hold the key to success and excellence, satisfaction and prudence. The teacher's role is simply to guide the learners as best as possible. In the process of guidance, she/he takes intensive care to see that each learner finds a favourable climate of efflorescence of individuality.

Apart from the fact that the learner is the teacher by herself/himself, a fact which is never ignored or averted in teacher education as Sri Aurobindo asserts, it is the role of the teacher to guard the learner against any mechanical or passive activity which severely affects cultivation of knowledge already in her/him. Simultaneously, it is also necessary that the teacher is very keen to provide the learners with every cue, hint or suggestion which would enable the latter to discover the ways and means of self-manifestation through self-endeavour and self-study. Self-involvement and self-activity, as Sri Aurobindo emphasises, are the essence of excellent education towards which every strategy in teacher education should be directed. As he categorically remarks:

> The first principle of true teaching is that nothing can be taught. The teacher is not an instructor or task-master, he is a helper and a guide. His business is to suggest and not to impose. He does not actually train the pupil's mind, he only shows him how to perfect his instruments of knowledge and helps and encourages him in the process. He does not impart knowledge to him, he shows him how to acquire knowledge for himself. He does not call forth the knowledge that is within; he only shows him where it lies and how it can be habituated to rise to the surface. The distinction that reserves this principle for the teaching of adolescent and adult minds and denies its application to the child, is a conservative and unintelligent doctrine. Child or man, boy or girl, there is only one sound principle of good teaching. Difference of age only serves to diminish or increase the amount of help and guidance necessary; it does not change in nature.[1]

As a foreseer of teacher education for better proficiency in teaching in order to enabling the learner to uphold subjectivity and creativity, positive and reflective thinking, Sri Aurobindo emphasises on education for development of individuality, and for that end-in-view, self-education and self-endeavour have no alternative. The real man within must be given a sound and healthy access and fulfillment within every learner. Accordingly, teaching should be meaningfully imparted.

The present day mechanical process in teaching should, as Sri Aurobindo reminds us, be eliminated and replaced by teaching for the efflorescence of inwardness:

> The discovery that education must be a bringing out of the child's own intellectual and moral capacities to their highest possible value and must be based on the psychology of the child-nature was a step forward towards a more healthy because a more subjective system; but it still fell short because it still regarded him as an object to be handled and moulded by the teacher, to be educated. But at least there was a glimmering of the realisation that each human being is a self-developing soul and that the business of both parent and teacher is to enable

> and to help the child to educate himself, to develop his own intellectual, moral, aesthetic and practical capacities and to grow freely as an organic being, not to be kneaded and pressured into form like an inert plastic material. It is not yet realised what this soul is or that the true secret, whether child or man, is to help him to find his deeper self, the real psychic entity within. That, if we ever give it a chance to come forward, and still more if we call it into the foreground as 'the leader of the march set in our front', will itself take up most of the business of education out of our hands and develop the capacity of the psychological being towards a realisation of its potentialities of which our present mechanical view of life and man and external routine methods of dealing with them prevent us from having any experience or forming any conception. These new educational methods are on the straight way to this truer dealing. The closer touch attempted with the physical entity behind the vital and physical mentality and an increasing reliance on its possibilities must lead to the ultimate discovery that man is inwardly a soul and a conscious power of the Divine and that the evocation of this real man within is the right object of education and indeed of all human life if it would find and live according to the hidden Truth and deepest law of its own being.[2]

Teacher education for a new role of the teacher in response to the above as Sri Aurobindo elucidates necessitates training in child observation. This will enable the teacher to allow sufficient exercise of freedom in learning through self-involvement and self-criticism to arrive at a point of learning correctly and learning for perfection of her/his knowledge and experience. The teaching of how children learn by means of cultivation of spontaneity and rejection of mechanical and dull procedures of imitating is the most effective of free progress of child education:

> In order to awaken the child to the understanding of the relations existing between the two worlds which he discovers almost simultaneously— the inner and the outer— he should be told how to observe carefully what happens in himself. He

> has to be shown that he is the playground, sometimes the battlefield of different forces and inner movements: senses, impulses, emotions, ideas. And he must be taught how to distinguish between them practically and find out their nature and origin. For this discovery intellectual explanations are insufficient, it is no use lecturing and moralising. It is with concrete instances, from the day to day school life, taking advantage of apparently insignificant incidents, that the discrimination can be slowly developed.
>
> The child will then be shown that it is possible to rise above the fleeting inner movements that he has now learnt to discriminate and not to be frightened by the inner silence in which he may enter—this silence that will later reveal itself as a plenitude.[3]

Sri Aurobindo's vision of education of the right kind provides freedom for the learner to grow in accordance with her/his own psychic process of learning without being hampered or dictated by the teacher or by anyone else. Teaching as an evolving process of transcendence as he envisions is very essential for cultivation of the ethical and aesthetic sensibilities. This allows the learner to learn how to prepare herself/himself to rise above the traditional concept of utility and be directed towards the principle of goodness that paves the path to inner pleasure. The teacher also cares for the learner's ability to, to uplift herself/himself from mere reason to a supra-mental state of consummation. No doubt, the role of the teacher to inspire the learners to understand and appreciate this transcendence from the aesthetic to the divine nature of the self towards perfection of inwardness is very challenging, but education as an evolving process cannot but stick to the principle of ascent and excellence of ethical and aesthetic sensibilities.

If the learner's freedom to learn is evaluated in terms of the above by the teacher, what Sri Aurobindo emphasises by 'the supra-rational good' becomes a prized reality in the evolving process of teaching-learning:

> Utility is a fundamental principle of existence, if one could find the way and be always sure of what is the real good of all. And though pleasure may be a sub-conscient motive to the pursuit

of virtue, the action of the ethical man is not motivated by even an inner pleasure, but by a call of this being, the necessity of an idea, the figure of an absolute standard. In the recorded history of our ascent this does not at first appear clearly, docs not appear perhaps at all: there the evolution of man in society may seem to be the determining cause of his ethical evolution. But that this is not the core of the matter is shown by the fact that the ethical demand does not always square with the social demand, nor the ethical standard always coincides with the social standard.

Our ethical impulses and activities begin like the rest in the infra-rational and take their rise from the subconscient. Man obeys the law at first without any inquiry into the why and wherefore; later on the reason labours to make us understand what the impulses and instincts seek after, but in the end these ethical ideas and this intelligent will escape from its hold and soar up beyond its province. For the ethical being like the rest is a growth and seeking towards the absolute, the divine, which can only be attained securely in the supra-rational. In fact ethics is not in its essence a calculation of good and evil in the action or the laboured effort to the blameless according to standards of the world, it is an attempt to grow into the divine nature. Such was the supreme aim of the ancient sages who had the wisdom which rational man and rational society have rejected because it was too high a truth for the comprehension of the reason and for the powers of the normal limited human will too bold and immense, too infinite an effort. It is with the cult of the Good, as with the cult of the Beautiful and the cult of the spiritual, the aim is man's rising from an infra-rational through the reason to a supra-mental consummation.[4]

For a composite endeavour towards following the ways of the intellect or knowledge, the heart or emotion and the will or action harmonised and shifted through a withdrawal within to become an infinite power in education as an evolving process as Sri Aurobindo advises for a culture of the super-mind, teaching should incorporate appropriate strategies for the exercise of four important steps: the higher mind, the illumined mind, the intuitive mind, and the over mind. The exercise of the super mind or the gnostic being thus enriched will lead the learner towards perfection in education.

What, in terms of the above, should be the role of the teacher in teaching children? Here is an encouraging and significant answer:

> The teacher becomes a guide pointing out how to become an animal, how to become a river, a cloud, an electron, or a galaxy. We don't have to disguise ourselves as animals, but we have to discover in ourselves that we are animals disguised as men, and at the same time men disguised as animals. We don't have to imagine ourselves being an electron, because we are electrons who imagine themselves building cells, who imagine themselves building a human being.
>
> The first result of such a continuous stimulation to identify oneself with a world in which there is nothing strange, nothing hostile, nothing other or non-self, is that we emerge into a universe where the only possible relations are relations of love. In such a universe even the virus which threatens the life of our physical body, as well as the lions who devour the gazelle, does it out of love. In such a vision there is no place for hatred. The only not-love is indifference, and indifference is the failure to recognise oneself in another.
>
> This true education is not an ignoring of facts. A true educator passes lightly over the facts because an intelligent child can get hold of all the facts he needs and will quickly find with the help of a computer everything men have known about the subject in which he is interested. The only thing the educator has to do is to awaken and stimulate that interest.[5]

As regards the medium and the instruments of teaching-learning, Sri Aurobindo stresses on perfection and development in right earnest. If the medium of instruction is alien to the learner, the teacher's purpose of teaching is greatly defeated. Again, the mental instruments like observation, reasoning, etc., require sufficient development the absence of which indicates poor teaching-learning.

The evolving teacher ought to give priorities to the importance to the above. As Sri Aurobindo suggests:

> The first attention of the teacher must be given to the medium and the instruments, and, until these are perfected, to multiply subjects of regular instruction is to waste time and energy. When the mental instruments are sufficiently developed to acquire a language easily and swiftly, that is the time to introduce him to many languages, not when he can only partially understand what he is taught and masters it laboriously and imperfectly. Moreover, one who has mastered his own language, has one very necessary facility for mastering another. With the linguistic faculty unsatisfactorily developed in one's own tongue, to master others is impossible. To study science with the faculties of observation, judgment, reasoning and comparison only slightly developed is to undertake a useless and thankless labour. So it is with all other subjects.
>
> The mother-tongue is the proper medium of education and therefore the first energies of the child should be directed to the thorough mastering of the medium. Almost every child has an imagination, an instinct for words, a dramatic faculty, a wealth of idea and fancy. These should be interested in the literature and history of the nation. Instead of stupid and dry spelling and reading books, looked on as a dreary and ungrateful task, he should be introduced by rapidly progressive stages to the most interesting parts of his own literature and the life around him and behind him and they should be put before him in such a way as to attract and appeal to the qualities of which I have spoken. All other studies at this period should be devoted to the perfection of the mental functions and the moral character. A foundation should be laid at this time for the study of history, science, philosophy, art, but not in an obtrusive and formal manner. Every child is a lover of interesting narrative, a hero-worshipper and a patriot. Appeal to these qualities in him and through them let him master without knowing it the living and human parts of his nation's history. Every child is an

> inquirer, an investigator, analyser, a merciless anatomist. Appeal to those qualities in him and let him acquire without knowing it the right temper and the necessary fundamental knowledge of the scientist. Every child has an insatiable intellectual curiosity and turn for metaphysical enquiry. Use it to draw him on slowly to an understanding of the world and himself. Every child has the gift of imitation and a touch of imaginative power. Use it to give him the groundwork of the faculty of the artist.[6]

The new horizon of teacher education ushers forth the role of the ardent teacher towards fulfillment of the mission and vision of education for the child from the living and purposeful perspectives of teaching as Sri Aurobindo has highlighted. The child must be the focal point of interest in teaching where the understanding, skill, interest and motivation as it demands out of its own attitude, aptitude and appreciation from time to time and from subject to subject under different climate of the pursuit of learning. Our approach as teacher trainees and teacher educators is to unfold before the learner a wide spectrum to cultivate as a thinker an illumined mind that cares for and unendingly nurtures perfect evolution. As Sri Aurobindo poignantly observes:

> The powers peculiar to this highest stratum of knowledge are chiefly known to us from the phenomena of genius,— sovereign discernment, intuitive perception of truth, plenary inspiration of speech, direct vision of knowledge to an extent often amounting to revelation, making a man a prophet of truth. These powers are rare in their higher development, though many possess them imperfectly or by flashes. They are still greatly distrusted by the critical reason of mankind because of the admixture of error, caprice and a biased imagination which obstructs and distorts their perfect workings. Yet it is clear that humanity could not have advanced to its present stage if it had not been for the help of these faculties and it is a question with which educationists have not yet grappled, what is to be done with this mighty and mighty element, the element of genius in the pupil. The mere instructor does his best to discourage and stifle genius, the more liberal teacher welcomes it. Faculties so important to humanity cannot be left out of our consideration.

> It is foolish to neglect them. Their imperfect development must be perfected, the admixture of error, caprice and biased fancifulness must be carefully and wisely removed. But the teacher cannot do it; he would eradicate the good corn as well as the tares if he interfered. Here, as in all educational operation, he can only put the growing soul into the way of its own perfection.[7]

When would we earnestly respond to the above in teacher education?

References

1. Sri Aurobindo: "A System of National Education", first published in the *Karmayogin* in 1910; reprinted in book form in 1921 and included in Sri Aurobindo and the Mother on Education, *Sri Aurobindo International Centre of Education,* Pondicherry, 3rd ed., 1966, p. 20.
2. Sri Aurobindo: *The Human Cycle,* Sri Ashram, Pondicherry, Chapter III, pp. 27-28.
3. Pavitra: "The Growing Child", *Education and the Growing Child,* Sri Aurobindo Society, Sri Aurobindo Ashram, Pondicherry, 2002, pp. 31-32.
4. Sri Aurobindo: *The Human Cycle,* Sisirkumar Ghose (Abridged), Sri Aurobindo Pathamandir, Kolkata, 1972, pp. 49-51.
5. Artaud, Yvonne: "*The University of the Future*—The Auroville Model", Education of the Future, Sri Aurobindo Institute of Social Sciences, Integral Education Series, Sri Aurobindo Society, Pondicherry, 1996, p. 36.
6. Sri Aurobindo: *"Education of the Child",* Education and the Growing Child, Sri Aurobindo Institute of Research in Social Sciences, Integral Education Series, Sri Aurobindo Society, Pondicherry, 2002, pp. 3-4.
7. Sri Aurobindo: "Intuition: The Faculty of the Future", *Education of the Future,* Sri Aurobindo Institute of Research in Social Sciences, Integral Education Series, Sri Aurobindo Ashram, Pondicherry, 1996, pp. 7-8.

10 Teacher Education and Education for Cultural Development: Exploring Dynamic Avenues of Efflorescence

Teacher education today is now facing a great challenge. It is the challenge of cultural development which almost every teacher necessitates to negotiate in every educational institution. For this purpose, as a sensitive practitioner in the task of teaching, she/he has no alternative but to be socially and humanely alert in the myriad forms of socio-cultural and socio-aesthetic ukase from which every learner more or less suffers and is affected by some sort of unavoidable alienation. The great challenge for both the learner-teacher or teacher-trainee and the teacher educator is how to enable the learner to be free from all forms of alienation which act as constraints to cultivate education for cultural development. It is a very delicate task for the teacher to teach on cultural efflorescence because it encroaches upon the sensitive mind of the learner who has her/his own way of interpretation, analysis, evaluation, appreciation and dissemination of culture. At the same, it invites social stigmas to discuss quite frankly where education by means of involvement of democracy in cultural sovereignty becomes a very arduous but fascinating adventure.

Keeping in mind the above scenario of teacher education, exploring dynamic and thrilling avenues of imparting education for cultural development demands a positive canvas for exercise in the backdrop of the following:

(i) As ours is a heterogeneous, problems-prone, ultra-modern, complex and confused society sans the much needed but very much ignored undesirably and blatantly personalisation, individualisation and humanisation of culture, it is time now or perhaps never to launch programmes for elimination of alienation through a well-defined and practical curriculum framework at every level of teaching-learning.

(ii) Education for a sane society sincerely interested in education for the promotion of culture can alone guarantee really cultured individuals.

(iii) Education for development of cultured individuals is assured only when the role of the teacher is directed solemnly towards stimulating the learner how to respect and endear neighbours, people of opposite sex, creed, culture, society besides those belonging to different ethnic heritage and culture.

(iv) To exercise education as a means of understanding, appreciating and sympathising with persons of diverse moods, tastes, habits, manners and customs is long overdue in our teaching for cultural development.

(v) The problems of self-alienation very often misinterpreted as a symbol of culture need arrest and elimination by means of education for cultural clarity of vision amongst young learners in particular.

Development of individual psychology in each learner for cultural enrichment is an uphill task for every teacher and, for that purpose, teacher educators are also trying to find out newer strategies for teacher training and orientation. The furtherance of development of individual psychology defines and explains freedom of culture through education and teaching in a complex atmosphere of social uncertainties nurtured directly or indirectly in educational institutions, thanks a lot to a different culture of indifference amidst an appalling difference between the high-ups and the low-downs, the rich and the poor, the advantaged and the disadvantaged, the ignored and the welcome group in an ever accelerating canvas of catastrophe!

As an unparalleled transmitter of culture, the teacher can make miracles in bringing about a total change in the mind-set of every learner in the cultivation of culture. How to be a role model for the learner to learn and refine culture that denotes humane development? Here is a suggestion. As an attractive and emulating manifestation of pleasing and educative culture, the sense of humour displayed by the teacher acts like a magic in the classroom. And that magic is nothing but the sparks of fine culture with which the learner refines and discovers newer avenues of cultural efflorescence and social enrichment.

> One of the most important qualities of a good teacher is humour. Many are the purposes it serves. The most obvious one is that it keeps the pupils alive and attentive because they are never quite sure what is coming next. Another is that it does in fact help to give a true picture of many important subjects. Suppose you are discussing English literature of the early nineteenth century. If you confine yourself to talking about Wordsworth's lyrical simplicity, and Shelley pinnacled dim in the intense inane, you will be giving an incomplete picture of the group; whereas if you also d-d-describe Charles Lamb as both f-funny and ch-charming, and bring out the weird boyish comedy of some of Wordsworth's other poems, and read some of Byron's rougher letters, you will then establish the idea that these men were rich and varied and human personalities, not "classics" cast in a single mould of solid bronze, and you can proceed all the better to explain both the nobility of their achievement and the sadness of their failures.
>
> Of course some subjects, notably the sciences, do not admit humorous treatment. There the wise teacher will continue to introduce flashes of humour extraneously, because he knows that fifty-five minutes of work plus five minutes' laughter are worth twice as much as sixty minutes of unvaried work.
>
> * *   * *   * *   * *   * *   * *   * *
>
> Humour must not be used to tyrannise a class. It seldom is so used. Usually irony and sarcasm are used, because they imply intellectual domination; but not humour. The real purpose of

> humour in teaching is deeper and more worthy. It is to link the pupils and the teacher, and to link them through enjoyment. A very wise old teacher once said: "I consider a day's teaching is wasted if we do not all have one hearty laugh," he meant that when people laugh together, they cease to be young and old, master and pupils, workers and driver, jailer and prisoners, they become a single group of human beings enjoying its existence.[1]

Teacher education always tries to uphold refinement and cultivation of culture through the teacher who is continually trying to introduce intellectual exercise in perfect sync with humane relations as the embodiment of social conscience. Let teacher education wage a war against a so-called modern society of drying aspirations and advancements in different crude and dull directions devoid of living and loving culture of togetherness and amity, peace and tranquillity. It is the sincere duty of the teacher and the teacher educator to orient every learner's intellectual capacity as an endeavour of development of the truly cultural being and not a mere learner toying with intelligence as a fashion in cultural exhibitionism. Education never eyes culture as a synonym for intelligence. Rather is it a force of intelligence—a very powerful force of course— that defies mere outward show but promises ascent and excellence unendingly. That the present level of human IQ must be raised is the forewarning of a compulsory and evolving culture, where teacher education cannot but correctly respond under socio-cultural and socio-aesthetic complexity in particular. The following extract clarifies this point:

> Some differences in degree of intelligence may be desirable, but the point is debatable and in any case the raising of the average nearer to the present maximum is evidently desirable. Such changes as these would require provision of optimum environmental conditions, but could not be achieved by this means alone; genetic selection in the existing variability of the species would also be required. There is ample evidence that intelligence is if not strictly determined at least strictly limited as to potentialities by inheritance. Even temperament is apparent to some degree hereditary and correlated with the physical structure, better knowledge of which would facilitate selection.

> Such changes, involving differences in distribution of existing characters within the human population, are evolutionary but they are of limited scope. Ultimate progress beyond these limits would necessarily involve the development of new characters in the human organism. Probably the new character most surely necessary for evolution beyond the present limits is an increase in intelligence above the existing maximum. Human progress depends on knowledge and learning, and the capacity for these is conditioned by intelligence. Most scientists are already aware that the progress of science is being impeded by the fact that the most brilliant men simply do not have enough learning capacity to acquire all the details of more than increasingly narrow segments of the field of knowledge. Only a very stupid person can believe that mankind is already intelligent enough for its own good.[2]

A new design of humane relationship prepared by the teacher devoted to developing finer sense and sensibilities of culture is the only alternative to arrest diffused and moribund culture writ large in almost every society everywhere. Unless a major paradigm shift in the vision and experience of education for the positive efflorescence of altruistic culture is assured in our programmes of action in teaching-learning, one might say we are simply weaving in the air in the name of education for development of culture.

The purpose of education for cultural development and, for that end-in-view, teacher education is to introduce the life of feeling as the one of the most characteristic components of education for development of the inner being. This is why all endeavour in teacher education should be directed towards the emancipation of the learner from all forms of alienation in cultural efflorescence. The role of the teacher from this point of view is undoubtedly very challenging because she/he ought to prove her/his worth as a teacher who knows very well how to be forewarned and obviously forearmed against automated programmes which gobble up all finer nuances of culture under the undisturbed slumber of passivity and disinterestedness. Professor Winthrop's observation in this connection may act as a sanguine guideline to the teacher in arresting alienation that eats up the vitality in teaching-learning:

> Only the human being can provide a sense of what a lived culture can be. This, he does, not only by example but also by bringing to the fore the importance of the dimensions of feeling and sensitivity for the human condition. Knowledge is not enough. One must distinguish, as Archibald MacLeish once put it, between a fact and the feel of a fact.
>
> Knowledge divorced from its significance for the life of feeling, knowledge disentangled from its social matrix to which it must have relevance, knowledge which does not determine the postures we take towards ourselves and each other can provide only an alienated type of education. This is precisely one of the greatest dangers in teaching by machine, for the automated program will frequently deal with abstractions completely alienated from the human context which gives them relevance. Alienated learning is a modern Frankenstein and it is tragically on the increase. Learning which cannot become part of the warp and woof of one's own inner being, is learning which, from the viewpoint of a philosophy of existentialism, is without commitment. Programmed instruction cannot escape increasing the fund of alienated learning and education in our time. It could be argued, I believe, that the central function of a great teacher is precisely that of preventing the process of alienation in education. In this sense he has no substitute and remains an eternal bulwark against the twin dangers of the Scylla of over-intellectualisation and the Charybdis of emotional and sentimental surcharge.[3]

Admittedly, in education in general and in teacher education in particular, training and development of culture have presented an altogether bizarre scenario in every institution of learning. This has its more aggravating situation in a pluralistic, multi-religious and multi-cultural country where some other delicate issues apart from the general ones have added more challenges to ward off curious confusions arising out of numerous problems of life and work, profession and vocation. Any culture and its thorough study from the standpoint of aesthetics of teaching in terms of education to be under a very favourable climate of emancipation of the inner man are maintaining a sort of unwanted distance which is to a great extent responsible for the downfall of serene culture, the paradise lost in the history of man the excellent.

The mission of teacher education for cultivation and efflorescence of culture is essential to prepare teachers by means of redefining the role of education in terms of pupil behaviour. For this the following come under critical scanner:

(a) The roots of ukase in the domain of theory and practice in culture should be scrupulously and meticulously identified.

(b) As soon as the task of appropriate identification is over, the task of the teacher is to cluster culture-components in order of preference, attitudinal attraction and appreciation from the learners' ends-in-view. It is to be taken into serious account that each learner has the unique capability to contribute to culture abundantly. As such, the teacher ought to introduce different strategies for different learners in accordance with the approachers to the most vulnerable areas of identity and practice in culture.

(c) Every training programme in teacher education for orientation of culture should primarily be assured of the fact that in returning to the roots of culture as an intrinsic or extrinsic exercise, two major constraints are always irritating and disturbing. These are finding the apposite means and solutions to our contingent and perennial problems, and the devaluation of creating the meaning, value and purpose of synthesis of culture. However, it is undeniable that a teacher in disseminating culture of the finest order emancipates a lesson from all abstractions, dullness and utilitarian points of view simply by her/his intellectual presence and credibility.

Teacher education for meaningful and vibrant cultivation of culture must guarantee efflorescence of humanistic heritage and tradition which endlessly contribute to the education of the complete man, the education that cares for sweetness and light. It must insist on delivering the truth that education and culture must at any cost uphold all avenues of perfection in unfolding the inherent moral, aesthetic and spiritual ascent and excellence in every human being.

The role of the teacher as an ardent exponent of mutuality of diverse and different cultures is legion. Teaching for that end-in-view also demands a continual and devoted pursuit of all the finer essence of culture from multi-dimensional points of view. In this connection one might recall the invaluable suggestions of Swami Vivekananda, the unparalleled connoisseur of education for the advancement of culture by means of spiritual consciousness:

> Wherever there is a thing really needed in one part of the world, the complement will find its way there and supply it with new life. This is true in the physical world as well as in the spiritual. If there is a want of spirituality in one part of the world, and at the same time that spirituality exists elsewhere, whether we consciously struggle for it or not, that spirituality will find its way to the part where it is needed and balance the inequality. In the history of the human race, not once or twice, but again and again, it has been the destiny of India in the past to supply spirituality to the world. We find that whenever either by mighty conquest or by commercial supremacy different parts of the world have been kneaded into one whole race and bequests have been made from one corner to the other, each nation, as it were, poured forth its own quota, either political, social, or spiritual. India's contribution to the sum total of human knowledge has been spirituality, philosophy. These she contributed even long before the Persian Empire; the second time was during the Persian empire; the third time during the ascendency of the Greeks; and now for the fourth time during the ascendency of the English, she is going to fulfil the same destiny once more. As Western ideas of organisation and external civilisation are penetrating and pouring into our country, whether we will have them or not, so Indian spirituality and philosophy are deluging the lands of the West. None can resist it, and no more can we resist some sort of material civilisation from the West. A little of it, perhaps, is good for us, and a little spiritualisation is good for the West; thus the balance will be preserved. It is not that we ought to learn everything from the West, or that they have to learn everything from us, but each will have to supply and hand down to future generations what it has for the future accomplishment of that

> dream of ages—the harmony of nations, an ideal world. Whether that ideal world will ever come I do not know, whether the social perfection will ever be reached I have my own doubts; but whether it comes or not, each one of us will have to work for the idea as if it will come tomorrow, and as if it only depends on his work, and his alone. Each one of us will have to believe that everyone else in the world has done his work, and the only work remaining to be done to make the world perfect has to be done by himself. This is the responsibility we have to take upon ourselves.[4]

Undeniably, teacher education for meaningful and reliable advancement of culture demands an all-embracing and altruistic approach to teaching-learning. Teacher education for the efflorescence of culture invites and welcomes every type of the learner's experience that contributes to broadening the horizon of consciousness. It caters to the needs of cultural development in every learner irrespective of any stage of education and the canvas of culture should be as large as the whole world from the standpoint of understanding and appreciation. Naturally, no straightjacket, oversimplified prescription for cultivation of culture at any level of teaching-learning is desirable. It affects the spontaneous and free response to different components of culture and both the teacher and the learner fail to be justified to the interpretation and appreciation so vital to the efflorescence of inner vision of serenity and catholicity.

Besides the necessity of teaching and learning how to be justified to culture as a means of development of the finer sensibilities that work upon all humane and aesthetic appreciation, the necessity of a genuine and unalloyed cultivation of intellect calls forth a feeling in every teacher and the learner harmonised with all richness of in-depth vision. Such a feeling nursed in the exercise of education as a true vehicle of culture is more than education as it is nowadays entrusted upon but one that steers the mind-set for an enviable attempt to remould the world as an altar of ever abiding and stimulating culture. A sense of self-willingness side by side with a sense of self-dedication to the cause of refinement of culture by means of teaching and learning for the advancement of human relationship makes the world our own, very own.

How can education be directed towards fanning the flame of the indomitable human spirit? How can teacher education be geared towards right thought, right analysis, right vision, and right appreciation of culture that stands for a perennial reflection of enlightened humanism? How can personal freedom be christened to register and activate human passion restrained by an error-free inner discipline and introduced in worthy accomplishments? All these and other related avenues of manifestation of culture should come under the umbrella of humane conscience and enrichment. Teacher education has no alternative but to seriously address all these issues in course of a well-planned design of activities well-suited to the teacher and the learner in tune with teaching-learning ambience.

Undoubtedly, teacher education and cultural development are concerned with a very broad spectrum of decentralisation in thinking especially in 'reducing or eliminating certain unbearable forms of social pathology' as follows:

> Self-development and the achievement of a sense of personal identity; elimination or reduction of existing and unnecessary forms of alienation; the achievement of a balance between freedom and authority; the inauguration of social, cultural and community pluralism, particularly in economically advanced, technologically-based societies; an increase in organic, face-to-face personal and community relationships; the encouragement of individuality and intellectual independence; the fostering of an increase in the variety of human interests and concerns; and the achievement of a High Culture as opposed to a Mass Culture.
>
> The establishment of small communities which can eliminate the social pathology traceable in whole or in part to excessive urbanisation; the achievement of small communities without sacrificing the cultural, educational, scientific, technological, social and material gains which are mistakenly thought to be functionally dependent upon rampant industrialisation and urbanisation; the reduction of bureaucratisation in human life; more direct participation by the non-governing voter in democratic decision-making; less brain-washing, manipulation

> and propaganda from our mass media; and the reduction of excessive organisation in industry and politics.
>
> A greater fostering of virtues of a religious existentialism in interpersonal relationships, such as authenticity, less role-playing, more genuine encounters, more frequent commitment to worthy causes and needed social programs, more actual involvement following commitment, more concern for and social responsibility towards adversity experienced by others and less bad faith in personal relationships.[5]

Decentralisation as a means of education and cultural refinement in encompassing all the issues under social pathology as above also insists upon doing justice to some other crucial issues in the human community. Every teacher ought to be aware of most of these issues because education and teaching-learning cannot remain passive to these components very often serving as challenges. Neither the teacher nor the learner remains deaf to these issues because these are always more or less active in the revelation of socio-cultural and socio-aesthetic behaviour of the learner. The teacher, too, cannot but respond to many of these issues because these are treated as spark plugs to cultural consciousness. As Winthrop adds:

> Less legal coercion in our lives and an end to the proliferation of legislation which tends to become rather early, on the statute books; less standardisation of social life and cultural diffusion; less central dictation and determination of social and economic values; less ugly urbanisation, less water and air pollution and healthier civic surroundings; and less waste of all sorts, whether through the unnecessary destruction of life in field, forest and stream, through the overuse of industrial raw materials whose finished products find no market, or other equally, important forms of waste, discussed by the present writer, but which are too infrequently emphasised in social criticism.
>
> More fellow-feeling or *geminschaftsgefuhl* in the human community; an increased use of the principle of voluntary

association in community relationships; an effort by educators to reduce the amount of suggestibility in human life; more and clearer personal direction in peoples' lives and a more self-conscious and consistent pattern of values; the reinstitution into modern education of the great, Greek ideals of paideia; a reduction of social prejudice, an increase of good-will and more community effort to increase the amount of international understanding in our lives; less fostering of local and regional provincialism by industry and the mass media; more economic planning to cushion the impacts of automation and cybernation and preserve the individual's capacity to maintain himself and family economically; and a genuine effort to get at the causes of war, eliminate them and inaugurate a continued, public education on the subject of war and peace through information in depth rather than through headlines, editorials and glib analyses over the mass media.[6]

Teacher education always looks forward to expanding the horizon of teacher enrichment in encouraging our young learners to be aware of some essential components of culture. These components build a strong and lasting foundation in preserving identity and tradition by means of sincere pursuit and unflinching perseverance. Some of these universal cultural values that come under the arena of cultivation in and through education as the International Commission on Education suggests in its report to UNESCO are as follows:

Awareness of human rights combined with a sense of social responsibilities. Caution is taken that rights are not separated from duties, that the concept human right is not imposed from a Western ethnocentric perspective but related to cultural traditions and national/regional contexts, and that the rights of individuals are linked to those of the collectives.

Value of social equity and democratic participation in decision-making and government, which will be the 'central objective in all parts of life'.

Understanding and tolerance of cultural differences and pluralism, which is a precondition of social cohesion, peaceful coexistence and conflict-resolution by negotiation instead of force, and ultimately of world peace.

A spirit of caring: A keynote 'value for future education', and an intrinsic quality of human compassion, which should be extended not only to the family members and colleagues, but to all the disadvantaged, the sick, the poor, and the disabled, for the well-being of humankind and our planet.

Co-operative spirit: While competition can be observed in all spheres of daily life, co-operation is all the more necessary. As the International Commission on Education headed by Jacques Delors observes: The world is our village: if one house catches fire, the roofs over all our heads are immediately at risk. If anyone of us tries to start rebuilding, his efforts will be purely symbolic. Solidarity has to be the order of the day: each of us must bear his own share of the general responsibility.

Enterprising spirit: A quality which is needed not only for economic productivity and competitiveness but for all life situations.

Creativity: Which will always be needed for technological advances, social progress, economic dynamics and all other human endeavours.

Sensitivity to gender equality: Which has been recognised as 'the key to development and poverty alleviation', and 'both a gateway to development and a measure of that development'.

Open-mindedness to change: Which will be the only thing which will not change, and the attitude not only to accept change but to act as an agent of positive change.

Sense of obligation to environment protection and sustainable development, so as not to create economic, social and ecological debts for future generations.[7]

A new platform for teacher education for promotion of a living and energising culture of altruism from the perspectives as above calls forth overhauling task force in teaching in accordance to a renewed and rejuvenated positive curriculum framework. Teaching is a culture by itself contributing to an intensive approach to coming closest to what stands for enrichment and refinement in the pursuit of culture. As culture to be dynamic and forceful must be an eternal fountain of new thoughts and promises to be translated through education of quality and excellence, the role of the tea becomes very challenging in identifying the actual mind-set of each learner in response to any lesson highlighting a specific component of culture to be exercised both in theory and in practice. There may be brilliant signs of progress in teaching for cultural awareness, but that does not provide adequate guarantees for its permanent interest and appreciation, reliability and sustenance in consonance with the changing approach to culture at every stage of development. What is of absolute importance for both the teacher and the learner is to utilise individual, independent and unbiased culture scanners with promises of poignancy and elegance in the continued enrichment of humane sensibilities.

Teacher education necessitates teacher preparation by means of introducing universal cultural values. For this every teacher should have a strong foundation of understanding and appreciating the culture of the East as well as of the West. She/He should also undergo training and orientation in the role of synthesis of culture and values of the East and the West, thus devoting to the study of the mind of man in terms of socio-cultural and socio-aesthetic values. The age-old traditions enriching human civilisation and culture everywhere should be emphasised in teaching-learning by setting newer agenda for incorporation in the curriculum for teacher education. As the Report to UNESCO suggests:

> The sensitivity to environmental protection was expressed in ancient China by the concern of the Taoists about the destructive consequences of technological advances to natural resources and their advocacy of 'return to Nature'. Altruism, originating in the love of one human being for another, has been respected as the highest human value in Asia for hundreds of years. Humanity in the next century must find elements of wisdom of Confucianism as relevant as it was long ago. Therefore, one way to foster universal values for future

centuries is to educate the young with great books of the past and inherit the fine traditions of humanity.

Another approach to the cultivation of these universal values for global ethics is to promote, by means of education, cross-cultural learning between Eastern and Western cultures. Culturally the East and West are compatible and complementary rather than contradictory and mutually opposing. The Confucian aristocracy ('scholar-official') of merit, rather than hereditary privilege, was closest to the ancient Greek idea of 'government' by the best'. Asia's cultural learning from the West has evolved from the material dimension (modern technologies) to the institutional (political infrastructure) and the socio-psychological (values and beliefs) dimensions. It is education that has provided bridges between Eastern and Western cultures. If and when the East and West could learn and benefit from each other, integrating each other's cultural thoughts—for example, the individual initiative with the collective team spirit, competitiveness with co-operativeness, the technological capacities with the moral qualities—then desirable universal values will gradually develop and a global ethic will be formed, which will be a fundamental renewal of cultures and a great contribution of education to humanity.[8]

The new global culture of humanity must come under the purview of teacher education with new promises and new ideals where the teacher really plays a very significant role in bring about a radical change in education in search of making a balance between human needs and human excellence to be manifested in every walk of life. It is really a very difficult task to formulate strategies in the necessary training and orientation of teachers, where the socio-aesthetic and socio-cultural enrichment of every learner should be considered in terms of reflective and evolving thinking along with the potentiality of evaluating interdisciplinary and participatory approaches strategies of development. Setting new agenda should, therefore, prioritise teacher education for emancipation of what may be termed as basic parameters of human freedom:

The basic human freedoms, freedom of thought and belief, freedom of expression, freedom of movement—which may be summed up as freedom self-actualisation and autonomous action—are the very anchors of world government. So, too, with the basic securities; security of life and property, security from arbitrary arrest and coercion, security from random violence. These have become the minimal foundations for all modes of association; and until they are recognised and secured, no world community can hope for stability.

* *   * *   * *   * *   * *   * *   * *

Under One World guidance, "the new exploration", as Benton MacKaye has called it, will begin: the assemblage of all existing knowledge and values towards the creation of an integrated plan of life. This new explanation has a wider province than the geographic one; but its application to the earth is important. For a survey of the possibilities of human existence, in a new ecological pattern, region by region, is the necessary basis for the resettlement and re-cultivation of the planet. That will be more than a reversal of New World habits: it will be a moral atonement for ruthless exploitation and desecration.

This new adventure demands psychological maturity, as the boyish heroism of old adventures did not; for it is an exploration of depth, to fathom all the potential resources of a region, geologic, climatic, vegetative, zoological, historic, cultural, psychological, aesthetic, and to assess its possibilities for continued human enjoyment and for further improvement.

Mankind has lived on this planet for perhaps a million years; yet many of the earth's potentialities are still unrealised. Much that has been overlooked so far has yet, for the first time, to be brought to light and properly valued. Much that was once coarsely violated, through ignorance or greed, will be restored. At last sufficient knowledge is available to rectify the results of importunate greed and to remodel an environment that had been degraded by the engineer's over-confidence in machine-made plans. When in seeking human balance, we go on to

> provide a balanced environment, we shall have, in most of the busiest centres of population, to undertake widespread acts of demolition, in order to restore, in a century or so, some of the basic natural ingredients for a full and rich human life. The notion that mechanisation and urbanisation, as they have existed during the last century, are subject to indefinite acceleration is a superstition foisted by those who have made the machine their God. A world culture, in establishing a common human norm, will not merely slow down these processes—it will often reverse them.[9]

The education for a look within is one of the primary and essential components of culture. Teacher education for cultural development should always provide ample opportunities for every teacher to bring about desirable changes in teaching for understanding and appreciating the inner life. Let the teacher and the learner be acquainted with the positive components of responding to the inner life. Let every form of response be a definite pointer to revitalise cultural advancements through continual refinement in strategies undertaken for every item of teaching and learning. This would definitely strengthen a renewal with as a means of education for cultural development. This would also open newer vistas of teaching for cultural integration. As Mumford observes:

> Once we have formed the habit of looking within, listening to ourselves and responding to our own impulses and feelings, we shall not let ourselves be so easily the victims of uncontrollable emotions and effects: the inner life, instead of being either a gaping void or a ghoulish nightmare, will be open to cultivation and in both personal conduct and in art will bring us into more fruitful and loving relations with other men, whose depths will flow, through the symbols of art, into our own. At this point, we can nourish life again more intensely from the outside, too, opening our minds to every touch and sight and sound, instead of anesthetising ourselves continually to much that goes on around us, because it has become so meaningless, so unrelated to our inner needs.

** ** ** ** ** ** **

> Man is both a symbol-maker and a tool-maker from the very outset, because he has a need both to express his inner life and to control his outer life. But the tool, once so responsive to man's will, has turned into an automation; and at the present moment, the development of automatic organisations threatens to turn man himself into a mere passive tool. Fortunately, that does not mean either the end of art or the end of man. What has happened is a momentary distortion of growth; and it is in the inner nature of life itself, after a period of growth, to seek to resume equilibrium, in order to be ready for the next act of growth.
>
> We are now at a critical moment of history, a moment of great danger, but also of splendid promise. The burden of renewal lies heavily upon us. Yes, the burden of renewal is upon us; so it behoves us to understand the forces making for renewal within our persons and within our culture, and to summon forth the plans and ideals that will impel us to purposeful action. If we awaken to our actual state, in full possession of our senses, instead of remaining drugged, sleepy, cravenly passive, as we now are, we shall reshape our life to a new pattern, aided by all the resources that art and technics now place in our hands. At that decisive moment we shall perhaps lay the foundation for a united world, because we shall aim to join together, not merely the now hostile tribes and nationalities and peoples, but the equally warring and conflicting impulses in the human soul. If that happens, our dreams will again become benign and open to rational discipline; our machine, however highly organised, will be responsive to the demands of life. And, in the end, proudly reversing Blake's dictum, we shall, I hope, be able to say: *Art elevated, imagination affirmed, peace governs the nations.*[10]

Education allows all forms of culture to be in perfect fusion with human tastes and temperaments, wills and aspirations for sensitising humane ans aesthetic issues in life and work. Naturally, the development of the right strategies for cultivation of culture for humane development by means of teaching-learning is an ever changing process of transfer and transcendence of higher thoughts, nobler visions, greater promises and superior performance in terms of a various disciplines to which it is always seriously attached. The new generation teachers for fine-tuning teaching for cultural development has really a very tough assignment in exploring the most suitable strategy that will ensure justice to the teaching-learning potential under varied situations and stimulating challenges. The culture of a true religion of humanity is one of the most fundamental ends-in-view of education. Teacher education, therefore, should be directed towards fulfilling all the essential components of teacher efficiency for promotion of education for excellence and quality in this direction. This will set forth new agenda for making a synthesis between culture and religion towards an ascent through spirituality and intellectual excellence. Thus a new spirit of culture will promise a new world of global culture of unity in an ambience of freedom and individuality creative and reflective thinking. As Sri Aurobindo adroitly spells out:

> A religion of humanity may be either intellectual, or else a spiritual aspiration, partly the sign, partly the cause of a change of soul in humanity. The intellectual religion of humanity already to a certain extent exists in the minds of a few. The fundamental idea is that mankind is the godhead to be worshipped, no other idol, neither the nation, the State, the family nor anything else, not even Science, ought to take its place. Man must be sacred to man regardless of all distinctions. And all this is not to be held as an abstract and pious sentiment, but given full and practical recognition in the persons of men and nations and mankind.
>
> The religion of humanity has already exercised a great influence and accomplished many things which orthodox religion failed to do effectively. Moreover, this religion has faith in humanity and its earthly future, it has largely humanised society, given new conceptions of dignity of the human being and opened new vistas of his education, self-development and potentiality.
>
> But still in order to accomplish all its future, it must entirely prevail over its principal enemy— human egoism, the egoism of the individual, the egoism of class and nation. These it may

> at present soften, modify, but not to give place to the love of mankind, not to recognise a real unity between man and man, the ideal which was first expressed some thousands of years ago in the ancient Vedic hymn and must always remain the highest injunction of the Spirit within us.[11]

The real unity of humankind, the culture of all cultures in education is not only one of the most essential and challenging arena of teacher education but also a promise for everyone associated with teaching and learning to be translated into reality. It also indicates a warm welcome to the world of devotion to intellectual and spiritual culture of the highest order. The culture of teaching the essence of excellence in an individual in terms of the common good of everyone everywhere side by side with the education of the culture of synthesis between inward and outward unity of man call forth a platform of teaching-learning afresh and anew. That platform is education for the culture of a spiritual religion of humanity:

> A spiritual religion of humanity is the hope of the future. By this we do not mean what is ordinarily called a universal religion, a system, a thing of creed and intellectual belief. Mankind has tried unity by that means; it has failed and deserved to fail. What is meant is the growing realisation that there is a secret Spirit, a divine reality, in which we are all one and of which humanity is the highest vehicle on earth and that the human race and the human being are the means by which it will progressively reveal itself here, with a growing attempt to live out this knowledge and bring about a Kingdom of this divine Spirit upon earth. To go into all that this implies would be too large a subject to be entered upon here; it is enough to point out that in this direction lies the eventual road. No doubt, if this is an idea like the rest, it will go the way of all ideas; but if it is at all a truth of our being, then it must be the truth to which all is moving and in it must be found the means of a fundamental, an inner, a complete, a real human unity which would be the one secure basis of a unification of human life.
>
> The higher hope of humanity lies in the growing number of men who will realise this truth and seek to develop it in

> themselves, so that when the mind of man is ready to escape from the mechanical bent, perhaps when it finds that its mechanical solutions are all temporary and disappointing, then the truth of the Spirit may step in and lead humanity to the path of the highest possible happiness and perfection.[12]

The new order and discipline that promises a new culture of human excellence in and through education is self-realisation of beauty. It is not only an aesthetic endeavour in education but also a culture that never makes any compromise with inanity. Teacher education for aesthetic and cultural development makes newer inroads to inner excellence by means of eliminating whatever acts as a constraint to the efflorescence of truth. The teacher as a living model of aesthetic sensibilities ought to encourage and inspire every learner to exercise her/his own depth of vision in realisation of softer feelings and finer thoughts for appreciation. Therein is inherent the joy and beauty in teaching as a true exercise of aesthetic culture.

In the backdrop for the above, for the exercise of aesthetics as a component of culture par excellence, Tagore's viewpoints as follows would always serve as an incomparable and ever assured guideline:

> In the history of aesthetics there also comes an age of emancipation when the recognition of beauty in things great and small becomes easy, and when we see it more in the unassuming harmony of common objects than in things startling in their singularity. So much so, that we have to go through the stages of reaction when in the representation of beauty we try to avoid everything that is obviously pleasing and that has been crowned by the sanction of convention. We are then tempted in defiance to exaggerate the commonness of commonplace things, thereby making them aggressively uncommon. To restore harmony we create the discords which are a feature of all reactions. We already see in the present age the sign of this aesthetic reaction, which proves that man has at last come to know that it is only the narrowness of perception which sharply divides the field of his aesthetic consciousness into ugliness and beauty. When he has the power to see things

> detached from self-interest and from the insistent claims of the lust of the senses, then alone can he have the true vision of the beauty that is everywhere. Then only can he see that what is unpleasant to us is not necessarily un-beautiful, but has its beauty in truth.
>
> When we say that beauty is everywhere we do not mean that the word ugly should be abolished from our language, just as it would be absurd to say that there is no such thing as untruth. Untruth there certainly is, not in the system of the universe, but in our power of comprehension, as its negative element. In the same manner there is ugliness in the distorted expression of beauty in our life and in our art which comes from our imperfect realisation of Truth. To a certain extent we can set our life against the law of truth which is in us and which is in all, and likewise we can give rise to ugliness by going counter to the eternal law of harmony which is everywhere.[13]

For revitalisation of culture by means of exercising the culture of the inner being, teacher education necessitates exploring newer horizons of teaching and learning the wholeness of being, the wholeness that starts with the lesson of culture in soul-consciousness. The education of culture that represents the quality and excellence in exercising how to harmonise the relation between conflicts and contradictions in life and work for a perfect vision of man the ever victorious in trials and tribulations is long overdue. The culture of mystery in education and the role of the teacher to enable the learners to unfold and appreciate that in terms of diverse experiences in different situations are also to be sincerely taken into consideration for appreciating the inner 'music' of man the aesthete:

> The touch of an infinite mystery passes over the trivial and the familiar, making it break into ineffable music. The trees and the stars and the blue hills appear to us as symbols aching within a meaning which can never be uttered in words. We seem to watch the Master in the very act of creation of a new world when a man's soul draws her heavy curtain of self aside, when her veil is lifted and she is face to face with her eternal lover.

> But what is this state? It is like a morning of spring, varied in its life and beauty, yet one and entire. When a man's life rescued from distractions finds its unity in the soul, then the consciousness of the infinite becomes at once direct and natural to it as the light is to the flame. All the conflicts and contradictions of life are reconciled; knowledge, love, and action harmonised; pleasure and pain become one in beauty, enjoyment and renunciation equal in goodness; the breach between the finite and the infinite fills with love and overflows; every moment carries its message of the eternal; the formless appears to us in the form of the flower, of the fruit; the boundless takes us up in his arms as a father and walks by our side as a friend. It is only the soul, the one in man which by its very nature can overcome all limits, and finds its affinity with the Supreme One. While yet we have not attained the internal harmony, and the wholeness of our being, our life remains a life of habits. The world still appears to us as a machine, to be mastered where it is useful, to be guarded against where it is dangerous, and never to be known an its full fellowship with us, alike in its physical nature and in its spiritual life and beauty.[14]

The education of culture and cultural development by means of understanding and appreciating the nature of the infinite in life and work is obligatory. Teacher education should introduce a new task force for this purpose so that education becomes a living and loving force of vibrant culture. If our teaching-learning can be carefully and sufficiently directed towards preparing every teacher as a pioneer in exploring the 'new man' who responds to creativity as a balanced and transparent, optimistic and confident organiser of culture and cultural development, certainly we would avert an unwanted crisis of character and humanity:

> *The capital act of the new man is an assumption of responsibility:* He does not transfer the blame for his personal misfortunes to his parents, his elders, his associates, his circumstances; he refuses to make his own burden lighter by treating himself as a victim of processes over which he could have no control, even when he has innocently suffered, for he

knows that in the moral life, future intentions are more significant than past causes. On the map that science and objective investigation supply him, he superimposes his own plan of life. So the balanced person treats his own situation, however formidable or threatening, as the raw material he must master and mould. But his humility, born of self-awareness, has another side to it: confidence in his own powers of creation.

Confidence in creation: A sense of the rich potentialities of life and of endless alternatives, beyond those that the immediate moment or the immediate culture offers. Confidence in creation, as opposed to the fixations, the rigidities, the narrow alternatives of the existing economic systems and cultural schemes; yes, here precisely is the deepest difference between the new person and the old who gave to external conditions and external stimuli the initiative that living organisms and above all living persons must keep for themselves. Those who have this confidence are not afraid to break with the existing patterns, however compulsive and authoritative they may seem; and they are not afraid to make departures on radically different lines, merely because they meet with rebuff or failure. Such confidence once existed in a high degree among the great industrialists who girdled the planet with rail road lines, steamships, ocean cables, and factories; and those whose task it is to build a new world on the ruins of our disintegrating civilisation must have that faith in even fuller measure. The new person, because he has not feared to transform himself, is capable of facing the world in a similar mood of adventurous amelioration.

Only those who have confronted the present crisis in all its dimensions will have the strength to repent of their own sins and those of their community, to confront and overcome the evils that threaten us, and to re-affirm the goods of the past that will serve as foundation for the goods of the future that we have still to create. For those who have undergone these changes, life is good and the expansion and intensification of life is good. To live actively through every organ and still

> remain whole; to identify oneself loyally with the community and yet to emerge from it, with free choices and new goals; to live fully in the moment and to possess in that moment all that eternity might bring; to re-create in one's consciousness the whole in which man lives and moves and has his being—these are essential parts of the new affirmation of life.[15]

The quest for the culture of being as the dividend of re-creation is the fountain of living culture. Education stands for that living culture. The teachers are the living promoters of that living culture. Teacher education, to be true, meaningful and purposeful, must be the living sponsor of that culture. The culture that brings forth identity in terms of creativity and freedom does not remain apart from unified and universal culture. Each teacher is self-assigned to the advancement of that culture in education. It should never be imposed. It should never undergo mechanical organisational and administrative design imposed by others. It should always be closely related to, if possible, entirely chalked up in accordance with, the ideas, principles and policies formulated by the teacher. The reasons are obvious. She/He alone knows the tastes and temperaments of her/his learner's response to education for cultural enrichment. She/He alone knows how to be directly or indirectly play the role of a co-partner of living and refreshing culture of excellence.

'The experience of fulfillment through wholeness', as Professor Mumford emphasises, is the true identity of a teacher in dealing with teaching culture that stands for enabling the learners to become splendid and genuine examples of 'awakened personalities'. Leaving aside occasional pitfalls and limitations which are nothing but signals for reorientation in the strategies of teaching for cultural refinement and balanced personality, the teacher marches on for the advancement of education:

> The experience of fulfillment through wholeness is the true answer to the brevity of man's days. The wakened person seeks to live so that any day might be good enough to be his last. By the actuarial tables he knows, perhaps, that his expectation of life at birth is almost three score and ten; but he knows something more precious than this: that there are

> moments of such poignant intensity and fullness, moments when every part of the personality is mobilised into a single act or a single intuition, that they outweigh the contents of a whole tame lifetime. Those moments embrace eternity; and if they are fleeting, it is because men remain finite creatures whose days are measured.
>
> When these awakened personalities begin to multiply, the load of anxiety that hangs over the men of our present-day culture will perhaps begin to lift. Instead of gnawing dread, there will be a healthy sense of expectancy, of hope without self-deception, based upon the ability to formulate new plans and purposes: purposes which, because they grow out of a personal reorientation and renewal, will in time lead to the general replenishment of life. Such goals will not lose value through the changes that time and chance and the wills of other men will work on them, in the course of their realisation; nor will the prospect of many delays and disappointments keep those who are awakened from putting them into action at the earliest opportunity. Nothing is unthinkable, nothing is impossible to the balanced person, provided it arises out of the needs of life and is dedicated to life's further development.
>
> Even in his most rational procedures, the balanced person allows a place for the irrational and the unpredictable: he knows that catastrophe and miracle are both possible. Instead of feeling frustrated by these uncontrollable elements, he counts upon them to quicken the adventure of life by their very unforeseeableness: they are part of the cosmic weather whose daily challenge enlivens every activity.[16]

The education of culture for goodness and morality needs a new approach in the programmes of teaching-learning. Gone are the days when the teacher delivered sermons in the name of culture of goodness. Gone, too, are the instructions that the teacher imparted on morality as an essential component of culture. Today's teacher education firmly believes that education for cultural development eyes morality and goodness from an altogether different perspective: such education cannot be *taught* but can only be caught. As such, the most ideal form of teaching culture to be justified to goodness and morality is to welcome and exercise an extended vision of our true self in terms of both these components. In this connection, Tagore's incomparable elucidation is very significant:

> An imperfection which is not all imperfection, but which has perfection for its ideal, must go through a perpetual realisation. Thus, it is the function of our intellect to realise the truth through untruths, and knowledge is nothing but the continually burning up of error to set free the light of truth. Our will, our character, has to attain perfection by continually overcoming evils, either inside or outside us, or both; our physical life is consuming bodily materials every moment to maintain the life fire; and our moral life too has its fuel to burn. This life process is going on—we know it, we have felt it; and we have a faith which no individual instances to the contrary can shake, that the direction of humanity is from evil to good. For we feel that good is the positive element in man's nature, and in every age and every clime what man values most is the ideal of goodness. We have known the good, we have loved it, and we have paid our highest reverence to men who have shown in their lives what goodness is.
>
> The question will be asked, What is goodness; what does our moral nature mean? My answer is, that when a man begins to have an extended vision of his true self, when he realises that he is much more than at present he seems to be, he begins to get conscious of his moral nature. Then he grows aware of that which he is yet to be, and the state not yet experienced by him becomes more real than that under his direct experience. Necessarily, his perspective of life changes, and his will takes the place of his wishes. For will is the supreme wish of the larger life, the life whose greater portion is out of our present reach, whose objects are not for the most part before our sight. Then comes the conflict of our lesser man with our greater man, of our wishes with our will, of the desire for things affecting our senses with the purpose that is within our heart. Then we

> begin to distinguish between what we immediately desire and what is good. For good is that which is desirable for our greater self. Thus the sense of goodness comes out of a truer view of our life, which is the connected view of the wholeness of the field of life, and which takes into account not only what is present before us but what is not, and perhaps never humanly can be. Man, who is provident, feels for that life of his which is not yet existent, feels much for that than for the life that is with him; therefore he is ready to sacrifice his present inclination for the unrealised future. In this he becomes great, for he realises truth. Even to be sufficiently selfish a man has to recognise this truth, and has to curb his immediate impulses - in other words, has to be moral.[17]

Teacher education for cultural development cannot but uphold the value of preservation of language because it serves as an instrument of culture. Whatever activities are taken up for imparting education for cultural development essentially depends on how the teacher gives importance to the language through which it is exercised. It acts as a strong force of cultural enrichment. The teacher recourse to enabling the learner to appreciate culture by means of diversity of language acting as a vehicle of synthesis as well as a component of diverse cultural identity. Indeed, education becomes the voice of a group-soul of humankind which is undoubtedly a rich dividend of cultural advancement through diversity in oneness:

> The seeking for a common language for all humankind was very strong at the close of the last and the beginning of the present century and gave rise to several experiments none of which got to any vital permanence. Diversity of language serves two important ends of the human spirit, one of unification, the other of variation. Therefore, it is of the utmost value to a nation, a human group-soul, to preserve its language and make of it a strong cultural instrument; a nation, race or life.

> What a distinct human group loses by not possessing a separate tongue of its own or by losing the one it had, can be seen by the examples of the British colonies, the United States

> of America and Ireland. Modern India is another striking example. It is significant that the one sub-nation in India which from the first refused, as much as it could, to undergo this yoke, devoted itself to a development of its language, made that for long its principal pre-occupation—that it is Bengal which first recovered her soul, spiritualised itself, forced the whole world to hear of its greatest spiritual personalities, gave it the first modern Indian poet and Indian scientist of world-wide fame and achievement.
>
> A common language makes for unity, and therefore it might be said that the unity of the human race demands unity of language, and that the advantages of diversity must be foregone for this greater good, however serious the temporary sacrifice. But it makes for a real, fruitful living unity only when it is the natural expression of the race or has been made so by development from within.
>
> * *   * *   * *   * *   * *   * *   * *
>
> Diversity of language is worth keeping because diversity of culture, of soul groups is worth keeping. In laying this stress on culture, there need be no intention of undervaluing the outward, material side of life. On the contrary, the inner and the outer depend upon each other.[18]

Side by side with enrichment of language for that of culture, teacher education in our country should highlight culture defined as follows:

> Culture means the total accumulation of material objects, ideas, symbols, beliefs, sentiments, values, and social forms which are passed from one generation to another in any given society.[19]

To teach Indian culture, the teacher must have a very strong foundation on the essence of the culture and thought of India prioritising mental culture more than material culture. This is to a great extent a consistent and sincere striving for the teacher to enable the learners to be justified to the enrichment of inner life more than the outer material one with utilitarian ends in view. This apart, the teacher allows the learner to appreciate and assess through creative and reflective thinking that promises culture of transparency and transcendentalism, and the ascent of man, where one is assured of the fact that culture replaces quantity with quality:

> When we speak of any culture, we have to ask one important question: What is the concept of man in that culture? Among the various cultures that have come down to us, we have two broad divisions: one, the Greek or the Greco-Roman, and the other, the Indian. In each of these two cultures, we see a distinctive view of man and his highest excellence. The concept of man and his excellence can serve as a measuring rod to assess the culture of a people. Apart from the material bases of a culture, which are generally common in almost every developed culture of the past—a certain measure of economic and social security through settled agriculture, simple handicrafts, and effective social organisation—the most important determinant of a culture is the direction of its mental life, the questions it asks of experience and the answers it receives. These stirrings in the mind of man signify the beginnings of a conscious and deliberate control and guidance of life's forces. This new trend in evolution could not have proceeded far, had man been subject to the pressures of nature in his external life. If he had to fight for his very existence, like the rest of the animal creation, he would not have developed even the desire, much less the capacity, to scale the heights of evolution on his own. Herein is the significance of his achievement of the rudiments of material culture. He can now advance evolution into the higher field of mind and thought; this is the special field of human evolution, where quality replaces quantity as the central criterion of progress. In this, he receives help from his unique capacity for speech and the transmission of accumulated experience. He is thus endowed with a cultural inheritance over and above his genetic inheritance. With the aid of these, the mental component of culture advances from generation to generation.[20]

To be justified to the above, teacher education for training and orientation of teachers should highlight the culture of quality enhancement in keeping with the socio-cultural, socio-aesthetic and spiritual evolution of man. As culture conforms and enriches identity and excellence, it is expected that the teacher should always take a keen interest in broadening the vision and mission of education for cultural advancement. Generally, there is a tendency to envision culture in the light of commercialism, utilitarianism, passivity and dullness, thanks to the hurrying spree for cheap manifestation of culture as a commodity. Amidst an unrestrained indiscipline and ukase in the present day life almost totally lost in bare living in inanity, the task of the teacher has increased a lot to stimulate the learner how to cultivate softer feelings and finer sensibilities which are the essence of true culture.

How to synchronise culture and development as a unified whole? How to broaden the vision and widen the canvas of teacher education for a comprehensive, sustainable, qualitative, transparent, altruistic and evolutionary process of humane development in terms of culture. All these and other allied questions at present come under the purview of teacher education for cultural refinement. It is time to rethink about the role of teacher education in bringing about a significant change in the society that harmonises different aspects of culture for a true emancipation of man. The quest for teacher education for dealing with the dynamic and positive principles of cultural cooperation is a new dimension in this decade of the twenty-first century is not only necessary but definitely obligatory also for quality and excellence in education:

> In general, the culture of a particular society is composed of three distinct elements: ideas, aesthetic forms and values, largely moulded by the traditions of the past and the aspirations for the future. Ideas give rise to habits and beliefs thereby perpetuating themselves through social institutions that provide stability; aesthetic forms reflect the artistic expression of a culture in its visual arts, music and poetry as well as the sense of beauty manifested in the day-to-day living of individuals and social groups; and the values of a culture are formed by the interplay of both ideas and aesthetic forms and

provide norms of conduct, standards of behaviour, and sources of faith and vision. Of these three elements of culture, the values are of the greatest importance; values develop the precious assets of wisdom and discrimination in a specific culture; and they also provide the dynamism for action and change, and impart vitality and quality to the life of the people. The understanding of a particular culture requires a correct comprehension of the ideas underlying it and a measure of intelligent appreciation of its aesthetic forms; it is, however, the values of a culture that contain its essence and offer the best way of understanding it and participating in it. A living and vital culture is rooted in authentic and healthy traditions, has the capacity of continuous renewal and adaptation, and is developed by new aspirations and bold innovations; in this way the past, the present and the future are reflected together in that life of the mind and the spirit that is the indefinable complex of culture. The humanities and the arts, the sciences and the technologies, the network of communications and relationships, the magic of poetry and the transcendence of religion, all these spheres of action and speculation form the pattern of a culture. The rich and fascinating diversity of these patterns is a precious heritage of mankind that needs to be preserved and developed. The participation of all and not only the privileged elite in the cultural life of a community, and the increasing cooperation among diverse cultures to renew and enrich all cultural patterns and to evolve a new sense of universality and a more harmonious and cooperative world order, these are the two great needs of our times that give relevance to the Principles of Cultural Cooperation and their elaboration, implementation and further development. The fantastic growth of knowledge and the rapid pace of change in all spheres of life make it necessary to initiate deeper reflections on the content of culture, the role of cultural values and the nature and methodology of cooperation. Such reflections should take place both inside each living culture and among them together in a spirit of cooperation and friendship. Those concerned with

> action and implementation should be able to forecast trends and innovate programmes of relevance to the future. The need for cooperative and inter-disciplinary research and meaningful dialogue is obvious and urgent.[21]

The culture of love in relation to the society and the self is one of the most characteristic components of education. Teacher education is yet to be appropriately justified to the culture of love as one of the fundamental assignments in educational institutions. Teachers hardly contribute to the development of the culture of love through application of intensive programmes of activities where she/he as a cordial partner involve herself/ himself with the learners. The festival of the culture of love in teaching-learning is a true pointer to advancements indifferent walks of life.

How to extend the sphere of the culture of love in teaching-learning? What should be the role of the teacher in bringing about a radical change in culture as a significant component of the excellence of one and all for fullness in education? Professor Mumford's poignant suggestions as follows are invaluable:

> To extend the domain of love, we must doubtless apply fresh psychological and personal insight towards promoting adventurous courtship, erotic fulfilment, marital harmony, parental nurture, neighbourly aid and succour. But while the renewal of all these phases of love is vital to the more general spread of gracious and loving ways throughout society, even this is not enough. Love is concerned, fundamentally, with the nurture of life at every occasion: it is the practice of bestowing life on other creatures and receiving life from them. Love is egocentric and partial until it can also embrace all the dumb creatures who unconsciously participate in the wider scheme of life, until it bestows itself on those who will never thank one because they are conscious of our gift or because they are unborn; until it embraces those who would do one injury, prompting us to treat them with dignity and generosity, as warriors in reputedly more barbaric ages often treated the enemy.

> So, it follows that part of our love must be expressed by our relation to all living organisms and organic structures; some of our love must go to sea and river and soil, restraining careless exploitation and pollution; the trees and wild creatures of the forest, the fish in the rivers, are as subject to our affectionate care as the dogs or the cats who live in closer dependence on us. Consider the systematic wiping out of the natural landscape and the withdrawal from rural occupations and rural ways that took place during the past century: the spread of megalopolitan deserts undercuts love at its very base because it removes man's sense of active partnership and fellowship in the common processes of growth, which bind him to other organisms. When such habits prevail, love is reduced to a thin verbal precept, not a daily practice—a precept to be cynically disregarded on more intimate occasions as well.
>
> For social and personal integration we must develop the small life-promoting occasions for love as well as the grand ones. Not a day, then, without nurturing or furthering life; without repairing some deficiency of love in our homes, our villages, our cities; without caring for a child, visiting the sick, tending a garden, or making at least some token payment of good manners on this common debt. But likewise not a day without some more smiling expression of the delights of love: generous evidence of what William Blake called "the lineaments of satisfied desire". Not just succour and service are the expression of love: beauty is its oldest witness.[22]

Teacher education for advancement of culture as the agent of change in the quality of life and mind-sets in tune with the richness of global culture needs a look afresh. That the twenty-first century teacher should be well aware of the enormous possibilities in education for cultural efflorescence amidst unprecedented challenges of crises of culture in different spheres of life and work is a really bold attempt to be undertaken with all devotion to duties and responsibilities associated with teaching at all levels of education for cultural development. The neglect of culture even now encountered in education for national integration as a definite component of cultural awareness calls forth an urgent necessity for overhauling teacher education through culture-enriching curriculum framework:

> Basically, the neglect of culture in the developing socictics arises from the loss of one's own roots by the ruling classes who are dominated by the values, attitudes and tastes imposed by the foreign rulers, and remain alienated from the masses of people. Much song and noise is made about national integration, but the barriers between castes, creeds and classes continue to confine groups in their own roots and narrow horizons. There is an urgent need to give adequate priority to culture in national plans of development.
>
> Apart from the neglect of culture as a factor of development, there is a serious problem of finding sufficient resources in conditions of scarcity and poverty. Admittedly, it is not easy to promote cultural activities and exchanges when all available resources are sorely needed for the basic necessities of life. The problem of resources is, however, often exaggerated. Both at the local and national levels the community can find sufficient resources if there is strong enough interest among the people and the necessary determination on the part of the leadership. Large amounts of money are readily found for science and technology; this is natural and fully justified. There is, however, no reason to starve research in such areas as education, the humanities and the social sciences, which contribute equally to the quality of life and the effectiveness of human resources. The arts and the crafts are not mere luxuries; they can generate creative work, elevate taste and bring people together in common endeavours. The spread of culture through appropriate policies and instruments of action needs comparatively small cost of money but its returns can be enormous in terms of popular education and the creation of that will to change without which development cannot gather momentum. We need to make culture an integral part of national planning, and this is rarely attempted in the formulation of national development plans by the elitist leadership of developing

> countries, so sadly estranged from the traditional cultures of their larger community. And in the affluent societies, the quest and quality of true culture give way to the claims of consumerism and commercialism, cheap entertainment and vulgar trivialities. A crisis of culture looms large everywhere and requires a new awareness of the good life and a true dedication to the [pursuit of cultural values, artistic forms and great ideas and ideals that liberate the mind of man and exalt his spirit.[23]

The quest for cultural excellence is endless and thrilling, persistent and promising. A true teacher knows it very well how to ignite the learner in the pursuit of culture as an inherent force for quality in education of the right kind and of the right mind well-supported and enriched by the right attitude and right principle of appreciation. Culture is, indeed, a matter of feeling, a sensitive fine-tuning of ideas and ideals as the learner thinks and acts, promises and performs in response to good intentions and illuminating exposures. The teacher alone can be an effective partner to respond and share with the learner in elevation of the different and marvellous components of culture exercised in and through teaching-learning as and when necessary.

The quality of culture indicates the quality of teaching-learning. A true teacher never discards quality in teaching and a true learner is never satisfied with learning sans development of culture. As such, teacher education cannot ignore the arduous and challenging task of preparing and orienting teachers in order to be responsive to the immediate and the long-term necessities of introducing appropriate, reliable and positive strategies for the learner's cultural enrichment. Training in co-curricular activities and researches on education and enrichment of culture should be an added dimension in this connection.

It is time to introduce newer plans and strategies for teacher education as a very significant agent of education for development of culture. Indeed, culture indicates one's real identity. It acts like a linchpin for a really culturally crystallised person. Teacher education that cares for cultural enrichment from diverse perspectives ennobles excellence in all directions of life and accomplishments. This is a significant phenomenon where rich attention is yet to be paid in teaching-learning: pupil-personality in terms of cultural advancement is the only alternative to arrest devaluation of values:

> in cultural matters, an assertion of personality is equivalent to independence and sovereignty in the political field. Nations want to be themselves. From this point of view, culture is the entire system of interwoven bonds maintaining this unity of personality. However, it would be superficial to consider that culture consists merely of the manifestations of a people's genius in art, music, dancing and building. Culture is more than that: it is a vast laboratory in which a special scale of values is elaborated and where the entire process of assembling the people's own elements of thinking takes place— the stamp which will be imprinted on all forms of artistic and literary creation. It is time we restored to the word "culture" its proper meaning and abandoned the restrictive definition which confines it to the periphery of life by imparting to it a flavour of diversion, amusement and hobby. Culture cannot be reduced to a mere evening at the theatre, time spent watching television, a visit to the museum at the week-end or a spare moment devoted to reading. It is intellectual values which distinguish man from other species and even from the wonderful robots programmed to imitate his actions. And culture is the crucible from which such values emerge, where preferences are formed and the hierarchy among them is established. It is a never-ceasing activity, demanding the collaboration of all generations and crystallising itself in axiological table which governs the entire life of society. It is impossible for a man to lead his own life by means of a foreign culture. Just as the stage of political independence prepared the way for economic independence, so both of them cooperate in a stage of development in which culture, which has been subjected to the constraints of dependence on the outside world, can manifest itself to the full, consolidating self-awareness, a determination to penetrate into history, the thirst for achievement and the hope of progress.[24]

Meanwhile, teacher education cannot but be aware of the aggravating disparity between culture and communication where the teaching of modesty in sync with a certain positive sense of maturity is more or less missing. The ever-increasing tangle between know-how and know-why comes at cross-roads to a viable exercise of culture in the arena of education in general and teacher education in particular. Unless the culture of mutuality is a lesson to be properly handled in teaching-learning, we have no way out but to be prisoners of indecision in education for cultural solidarity and poignancy:

> The disparity of our culture, and the communication block it has engendered, may have to be tackled on other lines. True, the method and language of science are not the same as those of the arts. Also, different sciences may speak different languages, even on occasion the same science may employ different languages, the wave and particle theory of physics, for instance. It is the same with the arts. A novelist may be stone-deaf, a painter may not be interested in reading books. These are facts not too difficult to verify. The way to solve the communication block may lie through a recognition of levels of reality and of a general framework. The solution will not come by either party, science or the humanities, claiming exclusive ownership of culture: science demanding that the arts should accept a second-class citizenship, while the arts sniff at the sciences as little better than workable but fallible formulae, a mass of know-how without any sense of know-why or ultimate purposes. As for the union of the two disciplines, that is likely to be achieved by only a few. After all, and fortunately, intellectual consent and understanding are not the only form of agreement and understanding known to man. We may be beneficiaries of culture in different ways, the difference need not divide. Culture means hierarchy, though hierarchy need not mean social injustice. All this might call for the restoration of rational inhibitions, an admission of degrees of knowledge, a sense of maturity and humility wanting on the modern scene.[25]

Today, teacher education for cultural advancement must take special interest in how culture grows and how culture is best represented by every discipline irrespective of its area of importance or significance whatsoever. A new wave of cultural consciousness welcomes teacher education that nurses and accentuates the evolutionary and radical thinking that adds to and enriches advancements in teaching-learning. As Professor Barzun characteristically observes:

> Fortunately, the quality of true culture is contagious precisely in proportion to its diffusion and its intensity. It grows as it goes, and the more it gets to be "in the air", the easier for teachers to galvanise others into educating themselves. No one can do it for another, just as no one can make a bad actor cry "Murder" with conviction—short of shooting him. How does education "take" and culture grow? When a man has been singled out by the Fates for education, what happens is that he first disgorges all the facts he has learned. He forgets on a really magnanimous scale. It is a spring cleaning in which he sorts out his true intellectual interests from the temporary or imitative. The true he pursues on a plan of his own, unacademic, no doubt, though not necessarily without order or system. Little by little, he takes aboard once more some of the cargo he jettisoned, but in new contexts and with a new command of his own ship. He rereads old books, thinks out again old principles. The work is slow and often unconscious, but it follows patterns laid down in previous instruction. This is proved by the instruction that an educated man ordinarily ascribes to the chance remarks or helpful hints dropped by this or that teacher. They stand for much more which lies below that surface. The whole reorganising of a fine and well-stocked mind may seem a haphazard, uncertain process; but it has its logic; it is an instance of thinking in the widest meaning of the term; which means that it is the working of a strong wish, early implanted—a passion— and out of it comes a characteristic work of art—a Person.[26]

That education cannot be neatly prearranged is yet to be christened in the hallowed platform of teacher education for cultural development.

The quest for the Person in the teacher is unending but adventurous, ever pursuing but patiently precious.

Do we believe and act accordingly?

References

1. Highet, Gilbert: *The Art of Teaching,* University Paperbacks, Methuen, London, 1963, pp. 53-55.
2. Simpson, G.G.: *The Meaning of Evolution,* Mentor Books, New York, 1951, p. 192.
3. Winthrop, Henry: *Ventures in Social Interpretation,* Appleton-Century Crofts, New York, 1968, p. 178.
4. Swami Vivekananda: *The Complete Works of Swami Vivekananda,* Advaita Ashrama, Kolkata, Mayavati Memorial Edition, 1989, Vol. III, pp. 171-172.
5. Winthrop, Henry: *Ventures in Social Interpretation,* Appleton-Century Crofts, New York, 1968, p. 429.
6. *Ibid.,* pp. 429-430.
7. *Learning: The Treasure Within,* Report to UNESCO of the International Commission on Education for the Twenty-first Century, UNESCO, 1996, pp. 244-245.
8. *Ibid.,* p. 245.
9. Mumford, Louis: *Faith for Living,* Ed. Sisir Kumar Ghose, Bharatiya Vidya Bhavan, Mumbai, 1965, pp. 73-75.
10. *Ibid.,* pp. 62-64.
11. Sri Aurobindo: *The Ideal of Human Unity,* Abridged. Sisirkumar Ghose, Sri Aurobindo Pathamandir, Kolkata, 1972, pp. 122-123.
12. *Ibid.,* pp. 127-129.
13. Tagore, Rabindranath: *Sadhana,* Macmillan India Limited, New Delhi, Macmillan Pocket Tagore Edition, 1983, pp. 119-120.
14. *Ibid.,* pp. 35-36.

15. Mumford, Louis: *Faith in Living,* Ed. Sisir Kumar Ghose, Bharatiya Vidya Bhavan, Mumbai, 1965, pp. 41-43.
16. *Ibid.,* pp. 43-44.
17. Tagore, Rabindranath: *Sadhana,* Macmillan India Limited, New Delhi, Macmillan Pocket Tagore Edition, 1983, pp. 44-45.
18. Sri Aurobindo: *The Ideal of Human Unity,* Abridged. Sisirkumar Ghose, Sri Aurobindo Pathamandir, Kolkata, 1972, pp. 99-100.
19. *UNESCO: Traditional Cultures in South-East Asia,* Orient Longmans, 1959.
20. Swami Ranganathananda: *The Essence of Indian Culture,* The Ramakrishna Mission Institute of Culture, Kolkata, 1965, pp. 23-25.
21. Kirpal, Prem: "Culture and Development— The Incipient Crisis", *Cultures*, The UNESCO Press and la Baconniere, Unesco, 1976, Vol. III, No. 4, pp. 86-87.
22. Mumford, Louis: *Faith in Living,* Ed. Sisir Kumar Ghose, Bharatiya Vidya Bhavan, Mumbai, 1965, pp. 35-37.
23. Kirpal, Prem: "Culture and Development— The Incipient Crisis", *Cultures,* The Unesco Press and la Baconniere, Unesco, 1976, pp. 88-89.
24. Malitza, Mircea: "Culture and the New Order: A Pattern of Integration", *Cultures,* The Unesco Press and la Baconniere, Unesco, 1976, pp. 98-99.
25. Ghose, Sisirkumar: "Two Cultures?", *Crisis of Crisis,* Bharatiya Vidya Bhavan, Mumbai, 1972, pp. 32-33.
26. Barzun, Jacques: *Teacher in America,* Doubleday and Company, New York, 1959, pp. 270-271.

11 Teacher Education and Reflective Teaching

Teaching is a matter of introspection. It becomes more introspective in reflective teaching because it gives more importance to finer introspection supported by creative and critical thinking. It prioritises doubts and problems to be greeted with a warm welcome in reflection by means of appropriate creative and critical analysis and evaluation followed by guidance and counselling for onward advancement in excellence and quality transfer. Moreover, teaching also demands some practice with information as evidence to the process of critical introspection. In teacher education, it is one of the most significant areas of teacher preparation by means of providing adequate and timely training programmes of activities in reflective teaching.

The most essential component that comes under the scanner of reflective teaching is the standard to be taken up for reflective practice in teaching-learning. Is the standard at crossroads with classroom effectiveness in reflective teaching? Is the teacher-trainee in a position to familiarise the learners with positive attitudes and approaches to reflective teaching? How far is the content matter well edited to suit the needs and priorities of the learner under the practice of reflective teaching? Are the teacher educators in constant touch with the regular programmes for training of teacher-trainees in reflective teaching? What are the teacher educators' major areas of assignment in training and orientation in reflective teaching? How to improve the content areas of teaching for the advancement of reflective thinking? Is reflective teaching a viable strategy for career-development as teacher-educators who by their own involvements as practitioners in reflective teaching set living and transparent examples for the teacher-trainees?

The challenges and dilemmas encompassing reflective teaching have of late stressed on quality and excellence in teacher education where the teacher educators, teacher-trainees, students and all others associated directly or indirectly with teaching-learning make a conjoint and communicated endeavour to make education primarily as an incomparable component of enrichment and ascent of mankind. The reflective teacher should be equipped with the following:

1. **Competency:** The three most essential components under competency are: conceptual thinking, analysis and scrutiny, and problem-solving.
2. **Commitment:** This essentially indicates how far the teacher is justified to teaching as a commitment to self-development and self-activity associated with reflective teaching.
3. **Encouragement:** Every teacher undergoing practice in reflective teaching should be christened in the spirit of being an eternal learner by asking the self, the colleagues, the pupils and the teacher educators in a family of teaching-learning. She/ He should also be aware of the fact that all true teaching is a processed, enriched and shared one focussing attention to excellence and qualitative improvement at all directions in any discipline under consideration.
4. **Prospects:** The teacher under reflective teaching should be assured with the prospects of searching for continued improvement in teaching-learning, analysis and reviews with a creative and critical approach sophisticated in fine tuning and scrutiny for innovation and improvisation and a positive march towards furtherance of more introspective studies and research as a mark of finer insight.

Teacher education is really concerned about reflective teaching because teachers interested in teaching for the development of reflective thinking very often suffer from some distinct dilemmas. These affect reflection and introspection, innovative thinking and creativity which are characteristic efflorescence of reflective teaching. These also affect the teacher's own motivation and interest, attitude and appreciation. These may be identified as follows:

First, the total personality of a learner as a whole or as a single one becomes a prey to confusion worse confounded in unrealistic and absurd strategies of teaching.

Second, cognitive skill development and the focus of attention to enrichment of creative and critical areas of the curriculum await clarity of vision as the teacher generally becomes a prisoner of indecision.

Third, maintenance of pupil-consistency in behavioural patterns as against flexibility and accurate response to particular items of reflective thinking become a common and unavoidable dilemma.

Fourth, catering to professional needs and priorities as against teaching from the standpoint of the personal needs and priorities of each learner under reflective teaching welcomes a series of problems very often detrimental to effective reflective teaching.

Fifth, whether the reflective teacher should be formal in his approach to teaching as she/he is in case of teaching in general or should be free and fair with the learner's own world of reflective thinking while learning a lesson becomes a major problem that necessitates sincere attention.

Sixth, in the process of reflective teaching, the teacher suffers from a dilemma of the reflective teaching topic-wise out of a stipulated curriculum vis-a-vis a subject curriculum catering to the needs of the society to which the learner belongs.

Seventh, in case of effective motivation of the learner, the teacher faces the problem of intrinsic and extrinsic incentives or rewards as a strategy for effective teaching for advancement of reflective thinking.

In addition to the above, there are other dilemmas that confront in reflective teaching in actual classroom situations, some of which are freedom and authority, individuality and preference, time-schedule, internal and external discipline, co-curricular activities and their linkages with reflection and critical assessment and so on.

Meanwhile, let us be aware of the fundamental characteristics of reflective teaching as a practice for meaningful teaching:

(a) Reflective teaching is to be pre-ensured with a favourable classroom atmosphere where evidence-based teaching well supported by progressive development directed towards higher standards is available.

(b) The process of reflective teaching should be a cyclic or spiralling one where it is a competency-based exercise in reflective thinking.

(c) Frankness, open-mindedness, seriousness, in-depth vision and pinpointed approaches by means of introspective analysis and probing evaluation are the hallmarks of advancement in reflective teaching.

(d) Reflective teaching expands and utilises the benefit received from exercise and enrichment of insight. This also paves newer avenues of insight development as a foreseeable process of finer reflection.

(e) The means and technical efficiency must be clarified in reflective teaching. It should also be pre-ensured with activity-based critical and creative approach as a viable strategy for intensive teaching.

(f) The role of the teacher in reflective teaching should be to orient and refresh anew the external programmes of teaching-learning.

(g) Reflective teaching believes in collaborative, conjoint and communicated approach in teaching-learning. As such, personal and professional teaching-learning are modified, analysed, assessed and implemented accordingly.

Teacher education for enrichment of reflective thinking idealises and exercises review activities associated with the existing research from the standpoints of relevance, utility and appropriateness. It makes a critical approach to teaching as an intensive means of gathering fresh points of view in synergies with analytical and evaluative skills that ensure a strong foundation of effective teaching-learning. Simultaneously, 'intellectual responsibility' as Dewey points out along with whole heartedness acting as 'an intellectual force' for consolidated interest in the process of reflective thinking becomes the watch-tower of reflective teaching:

> There is no greater enemy of effective thinking than divided interest. * * * * A genuine enthusiasm is an attitude that operates as an intellectual force. When a person is absorbed, the subject carries him on.[1]

Reflection in action is crucial to the success of reflective teaching. All our direct experiences must be scanned under the adjustments that take place in teaching-learning. The teacher in such a process of reflective teaching constructs a theory of her/his own, frames a problem-based solution quite unique in character and employs in an interactive classroom situation thereby expanding the horizon of reflective teaching. In the words of Professor Schon:

> When someone reflects-in-action, he [sic] becomes a researcher in the practice context. He is not dependent on the categories of established theory and technique, but constructs a new theory of the unique case. He does not keep means and ends separate, but defines them interactively as he frames a problematic situation. He does not separate thinking from action.[2]

Planning, making provision, acting, collecting apposite evidence, analysing and assessing evidence followed by reflection—all these steps indicate the right approach to reflective teaching. A reflective teacher-trainee, under the guidance and supervision of concerned teacher educators already proves her/his worth in processing the seven-fold strategy of reflective teaching in a simulated classroom teaching where the inputs of all associated with the lesson provide necessary feedback for improvement of reflective teaching. Sometimes the teacher's intuition plays an inspiring part in enriching the reflective practice. But intuition also presupposes a rich background of ideas and experiences associated with a definite pattern of arrangements in reflective thinking.

A reflective teacher always expects some essential components in teaching for better efflorescence in reflective thinking. The first point of expectation in this connection is that the class is as less structured as possible for better avenues of individuality by means of independent learning. Secondly, the teacher enjoys some sort of satisfaction in briefing individual learners by becoming a partner to learning. The learner, too, finds a favourable climate of exercise in reflective thinking. Thirdly, how far the reflective teacher is successful in upholding the democratic approach without disturbing the exercise expected in individual thinking becomes a real challenge in teaching for the development of reflective thinking. Fourthly, is it possible that all the students come under a common fold of reflective thinking, and even it is possible, is it at all desirable because it greatly affects individual thinking and, as such, reflection has a tendency to be arrested in passivity which is a product of drabness and affects the finer zones of intelligence and appreciation.

If teaching is, as we cannot but admit, a public activity more prone to be histrionic than anything else, it calls forth an uninterrupted and alert vigilance on the part of the reflective teacher who is none but a smart actor in the ever changing process of teaching-learning. Is the teacher always ready to utilise the self looking glass? If so, how far is the looking glass dependable? Again, if the glass is more conscious of the self-image what should the role of the teacher in extinction of personality? And, if extinction of personality remains absent from teaching, can it be really reflective teaching in the true sense of the term?

Competition and contrast are the key factors in reflective teaching. Under the present classroom climate available or negotiable almost in every educational institution everywhere, the reflective teacher simply weaves in the air in launching programmes of action because competition becomes numerical rather than qualitative. Again, competitions very often grab the potentiality and potency so inseparable and vital in the culture of reflective teaching. Even some classes in the form of reflective teaching becomes more involved in competition in the strategy of silence as a plus point of reflective enrichment. But that undesirably welcomes issues pertaining to the assignment of teaching reflective or otherwise. Who understands the reflective teacher who hardly teaches but always learns?

A reflective teacher is fundamentally at crossroads with two very typical positions— the core identity and the professional identity. These two different identities— the substantive and the situated—make a very embarrassing situation in reflective teaching where it is very difficult to be justified to both. It is also very difficult to ignore both and become radical in reflective endeavour as an incomparable individual teacher because it is branded as an alienated adventure without any specific and structured end-in-view. Ironically, skills and informations in today's world of teaching-learning care everything else unnecessary and redundant, reflective enrichment notwithstanding.

Again, when we say that reflective teaching is free from any structure, it is not absolutely true because all thinking from the teacher's end are somehow or other more or less structured in the arrangement of thinking initially. This may be different in different cases under different teaching climate also from the point of view of aptitude. This also varies under different time schedules. Bearing in mind, the reflective teacher is always conscious of the needs and priorities of a comprehensive and arresting structure to put all teaching strategies in perfect gear as the class responds to a topic to be taught through administering reflective teaching strategies.

The role of the reflective teacher as above necessitates self-awareness. In teacher education, the role of the teacher-educator is to inspire and enable the reflexive teacher practitioner not only to train her/him in the reflective strategies in teaching but also to make her/him very careful and conscious of the ongoing process of reflective practice. How to create a helping relationship between the teacher and the teacher trainee and the students under the fold of reflective practice through self-consciousness is a very challenging activity. Here is a strategy Francis adopted to show how there is a mismatch between 'espoused theories of practice' and 'choice of metaphors' among the beginning teacher practitioners in reflective teaching on story telling:

> I see myself as a teacher who is like a current flowing through an electric circuit. Each student causes a resistance and a subsequent withdrawal of energy from the teacher. ... the source of energy which the teacher relies on eventually runs down and needs to be recharged if the light bulbs are to continue to glow brightly. [2]

The teacher educator might introduce a few strategies best suited to the reflective teaching practitioner for development of self-awareness . One of the dependable strategies is to introduce individual or group activities where the following points are really interesting and thought-provoking:

(a) You are very new to the teaching profession.

After some very early experiences in the classroom, think about your answers to the questions below. Then share your thoughts with other beginning teachers after attempting to answer the following questions:

- What kind of status does teaching have?
- What does it mean to you, personally, to take on the mantle of 'teacher'?
- What public images are there of teachers with which you can identify?
- How might new teachers begin to combine their personal and professional identities? (Accept that, for some, this might be experienced as the inability to be oneself).
- What is your overall philosophy of teaching and learning?
- What assumptions (implicit or explicit) about the nature of students' learning are inherent in your approaches to teaching?

(b) Try to return to the final two questions in three and, then, six months' time and answer them again.

- What changes to your philosophy and your assumptions have taken place?
- Specifically, have there been any changes to your general approach to teaching and learning, for example, in terms of you 'reaching out' to all the students in your classes?[3]

In teacher education, the teacher educator has an arduous responsibility in enabling the teacher practitioner to develop her/his skills of judgement. Peer team work becomes very effective for this purpose. The major areas that come under the fold of exploration in a learning conversation may be identified as stimulus, responsibility, information, ethical problems, cultural and linguistic problems, consequences and agreement. The sources of judgement, the positive reasons thereof, the negative constraints, information schedules, clarifications about the validity of informations, justifications, analytical assessments on agreement, disagreement, conflict and indifference—all these and other allied factors that contribute to a great extent in reflective thinking in the development of skills of judgement. It is to be noted that the teacher educator is also a regular and constant contributor in the process of participation in reflective thinking and writing.

The role of the teacher in the development of reflective thinking is legion. She/He must be self-assured of the fact that there is a danger of reducing reflective teaching into a set of procedures. That it is never a mechanical process in teaching but is always evolving with newer and more diverse paradigms in teaching can hardly be overestimated. It is never equivalent to a set pattern of standardised practices in the name of critically assessing competency. The question that should always prompt the reflective teacher is: Am I in a sound position to believe and act accordingly that reflection is a spontaneous and endless habit of deliberate and free-thinking in creative power of efflorescence?

The changing role of critical reflection necessitates proper vigilance and fitting guidance as the reflective practitioner chalks out of her/his strategies of thinking in teaching a particular item. Here two factors clash against independent reflective patterns of teaching: one, the socially dominant reflective thinking, and the second, the individual teacher's own map of reflection. How far is the reflective teacher free to exercise reflective thinking? Who will be the final decision maker, and why?

To move from changed awareness to changed practice as often thrust upon a reflective practitioner invites anomalies often disturbing and affecting better reflective practice. The problems that the teacher faces in teaching for reflective thinking are primarily the clash between teaching for understanding and teaching for appreciation, the set-patterns of the learners' own ideas and interpretations and the finer issues that require in-depth analysis and appreciation, and, last but not the least, an apposite assessment.

Team work in reflective teaching is now-a-days a common phenomena irrespective of its plus and minus points. That it is the most viable and dependable form of reflective teaching for advancement of creative and critical appreciation is subject to some reservations. Apart from the fact that no reflective teaching remains innovative and original under the umbrella of team work in reflective teaching is absolutely undeniable.

Besides the above, there are other issues which seriously hamper reflective teaching-learning:

(a) In team work and team teaching, very important and complex components under reflective analysis and appreciation are lost in the digressive discussions among peer groups where the reflective teacher very often fails to maintain balanced thinking and expression due to undesirable and unavoidable constraints.

(b) In the name of team teaching for reflective exercise, the role of all the teachers remains under dubious scanner. This type of reflective teaching allows undue flexibility and freedom that severely affects indiscipline in the name of teaching assignment.

(c) When there is team work in reflective teaching, the voice of the individual learner under active participation becomes a myth and never a stimulating reality. There is neither a way in nor a way out for the reflective practitioner to revise or reorient the already scheduled programme for team work.

(d) The desirable climate for team-working in reflective teaching is hardly available. As such, team is the dream child as it were of teaching and reflection a romantic ideal with neither a sound beginning nor a consolidated and promising step to fruitful ends-in-view.

(e) The problem of psychological complexities under the twin banner of inferiority and superiority complex can scarcely be averted.

Collaborative teaching for enrichment in reflective thinking is also very delicate in the teaching of humanities and fine arts where collaboration shortens the span of deep reflection and subjective vision. Reflective teaching is not meant for cognition because it is simply a pre-condition to the learner. As soon as the window of meta-cognition is wide open, the reflective teacher gets the entry into the world of reflective teaching where the other finer components of reflective teaching wait for apposite projection by means of creative, aesthetic and critical exercise.

Collaborative teaching for development of reflective exercise is a supportive affair. The question is: Is reflective teaching supportive? If it is so, what about creative and critical thinking and appreciation? Again, if we rely on collaborative thinking, are we assured of the fact that it will not affect or encroach upon independent creative and reflective exercise?

To frame or/and re-frame sets of supportive materials in accordance with the reflective patterns of thinking invite many constraints which cannot be left aside. Besides, in such collaborative endeavour, there are ample opportunities for undertaking a parasitical approach where teaching for reflective thinking becomes a headache of the few overpowering or belittling others as colleagues in the names of reflective teachers. This has its effect upon learners also. They simply brand reflective teaching either as a refuge for the truants or as a veritable exercise for highlighting authoritarianism in the name of reflective teaching.

Admittedly, reflective teaching always entertains serious issues. If the teacher fails to negotiate all the issues with their genuineness in enrichment of reflective thinking, the whole purpose of teaching for development of reflective thinking is greatly defeated. To look for possible or definite way out from such issues is to refine collaborative teaching which requires appropriate guidance and supervision. In teacher education this becomes a very hard nut to crack. The reasons are as follows:

(a) Collaborative reflective teaching is more or less a failure to understand and appreciate the pitfalls of very sensitive reflective learner practitioners.

(b) The practice under collaboration in reflective teaching most often makes the reflective practitioner imprisoned in the culture of already known areas of teaching where innovative practice has practically no entry or contribution.

(c) Under stipulated exercise in reflective teaching, the reflective practitioner does not care about freedom to be as one ought to be. As such, this affects the promising reflective teacher professionally.

(d) The teaching sessions for reflective teaching are very often strictly time-bound. This often breaks the set-pattern of the reflective practitioner in introducing newer designs and strategies for reflective exercise.

(e) In collaborative exercise of reflective teaching, the reflective practitioner has no alternative but to follow the set-pattern of exercise for classroom motivation. As motivation varies from learner to learner in reflective teaching, leaving aside the fact that compulsory motivation is not at all congenial to the highly reflective and gifted learner, its role in the advancement of reflective thinking under collaborative reflective teaching is very often dubious and negative.

Any change in collective practices related to reflective teaching means a total renewal of the plans and programmes in reflective teaching. This is a very challenging and time consuming activity. Moreover, one cannot be assured of the effectiveness of a changed programme in a re-framed setting for reflective teaching for those who are advanced learners because the latter might significantly be more conscious of their own contributions to reflective, in-depth, independent, creative and critical vision which they want to retain absolutely free and unaffected by any revised programme of guidance and supervision very often unduly thrust upon them.

The reflective practitioner in teaching might take recourse to reorganising the entire programme of teaching by considering the following suggestions:

(a) *Fool-proof response to pupil diversity in exercise of reflective thinking.*

All learners exercising reflective thinking are diversified personalities. They are interested in reflective thinking from different perspectives, the role of the teacher practitioner in reflective teaching is to properly identify the needs and priorities of identifying each and every component of pupil diversity in reflective thinking. Otherwise, the whole purpose of involving the learner in the exercise of reflective thinking will be greatly affected by mechanical and passive teaching-learning.

(b) *Improving Quality of Teaching-learning.*

A reflective teacher cannot make any compromise with teaching that fails to improve quality from time to time and from pupil to pupil. The first and foremost duty and responsibility of the reflective practitioner is to be assured of maintaining and accelerating quality of pupils' reflective thinking. This may be possible by a study of the pupil assessment of reflective teacher profile received from the reflective learners from time to time, which may be reviewed by the teacher educator(s) concerned. This may further be scanned by the reflective teacher's self-assessment profile in order to arrive at a definite point of improvement of the teaching strategies of the reflective practitioner. The process of critical reflection as Fook (2000) in the study of social work has suggested for forming reflective group structure is an effective participatory and reliable process in the advancement of reflective thinking. It also focusses our attention to the two major ends-in-view of reflective teaching viz., why and what to do.

In the advancement of reflective teaching, the role of the reflective practitioner is great. It is to be noted that no teaching is effective unless it is rich and challenging, critical and creative. In teacher education, these essential qualities are indicators to a welcome change in the traditional assignments of teachers in the process of teaching. As Professor Loughran characteristically observes:

> It does not divorce feelings from the actions associated with confrontation or challenge; it creates powerful learning episodes. * * * Working with colleagues * * * (provides the opportunity) of gaining advice and feedback on such episodes and of continuing to push to make the tacit explicit.[5]

What, then, should be the quality of a reflective practitioner in the enrichment of teaching for development of reflective thinking? Here is a classic suggestion:

> "In his classroom he [William James] was precisely what he was everywhere else—just as unorganised, just as stimulating

and irresistibly charming." He found it impossible to make a long, sustained, orderly, authoritative speech and to unfold, stage by stage, argument by argument, proof by irresistible proof, a philosophical theory. He felt that any such speech would stiffen and cripple the essential flexibility of thought, and that any such theory must misrepresent the infinite complexities and novelties and inconsistencies of reality. It was wrong, he felt, to tell people things. He would rather add "if" or "may be"; he would interrupt himself to catch a fleeting suggestion and come back saying "What was I talking about?" He created objections to his own proposals, he preferred discussion to straight oratory, and he made jokes on the most solemn subjects, very much as life itself does. Once he read out Spencer's definition of evolution:

> Evolution is an integration of matter and concomitant dissipation of motion; during which the matter passes from an indefinite, incoherent homogeneity to a definite, coherent heterogeneity.

And then he translated it:

> Evolution is change from a no-howish, untalk about able, all-alikeness to a somehowish and in general talk about able not-all-alikeness by continuous stick-togetherations and something-elsifications.

He even projected the grimmest problem of all, the problem of evil, withimpish realism rather than professional logic, by telling a class:

> This universe will never be completely good as long as one being is unhappy, as long as one poor cockroach suffers the pangs of unrequired love.

And we can imagine what horror he aroused in Harvard by remarking: "God is certainly no gentleman." Yet everyone knew that through his naughtiest flippancies as through his most puzzling incoherences there pulsed the genuine warmth which comes from the heart of life.[6]

When would teaching be ignited with 'the genuine warmth' in the arena of teacher education for development of reflective teaching?

References

1. Dewey, J: *How We Think: A Restatement of the Relation of Reflective Thinking to the Educative Process,* Henry Regnery, Chicago, 1933, p. 30.
2. Francis, D.: *'The reflective journal: a window to pre-service teachers' practical knowledge',* Teaching and Teacher Education, Vol. XI, No. 3, p. 229.
3. Dymoke, Sue and Harrison, Jennifer: *Reflective Teaching and Learning,* Sage, South Asia Edition, 2010, pp. 16-17.
4. Fook, J. : *Social Work: Critical Theory and Practice,* Sage, London, 2000.
5. Loughran, J.: *Developing a Pedagogy of Teacher Education, Understanding Teaching and Learning about Teaching,* Routlege, London, 2006, p. 57.
6. Highet, G: *The Art of Teaching,* Methuen, London, 1963, pp. 205-206.

12 Teacher Education and Tutoring

Teacher education in the twenty first century is opening newer dimensions and possibilities in the enrichment of teaching-learning. It has spread its vast canvas by welcoming newer directions in the advancement of better teaching through a series of openings so that learning becomes an attractive and interesting activity and, at the same time, the teacher by profession becomes assured of initial preparation desirable from the learners' end. Hence, tutoring has taken a major role in formulating and extending the horizon of teacher education.

Tutors are normally those who are not professional teachers. They are not directly associated with teaching as we come across in an institution of teaching-learning. Their role is a supportive and interacting one. In discharging their role it is expected that they maintain a cordial relationship with professional teachers in order to make teaching meaningful, purposeful, relevant, interesting and assertive. Moreover, with successful tutoring, the professional teacher finds a very favourable and positive classroom climate because the learners are in a position to follow the lesson easily and spontaneously without facing initial constraints in particular.

Who are the tutors? Anyone can be a tutor. To prepare a common list of tutors, the following would be included:

- Parents/Guardians,
- Sisters/Brothers,
- Adult Caretakers,
- Volunteers, and
- Peers,
- Others not directly associated as professionals in teaching.

Tutoring is nothing new. It dates back from ancient Rome and Greece. In our country, a more or less tutoring is performed by grandparents even now in joint families. To be a tutor does not necessarily demand one to be an expert in skill or subject-matter. But it definitely demands an obligation to make the tutee-learner initially equipped in understanding and appreciating professional teachers in the educational institution to which she/he is attached.

Effective tutoring contributes a lot to advancement in teacher education. Compared to professional teaching, it stimulates the tutee-learner profusely. As Professor Topping observes, it welcomes:

- more practice,
- more activity and variety,
- more individualised help,
- more questioning,
- simpler vocabulary,
- more modelling and demonstration,
- more local relevant examples,
- higher disclosure of misunderstanding,
- more prompting and self-correction,
- more immediate feedback and praise,
- more opportunities for generalisation,
- more insight into learning (meta-cognition), and
- more self-regulation and ownership of the learning process.[1]

To make tutoring really very effective, teacher education should provide opportunities for training and orientation in the different skills which would enable them to make tutoring more enjoyable and worthwhile to the learners. Professor Topping suggests some very essential and practical points:

Consistent and regular time: Tutor and tutee must agree how much time they can give to working together. How often will you meet each week? How long is each session? Over how many weeks? Where? Do not start anything you cannot keep up or finish. Regular meetings are needed to build up a trusting and comfortable tutoring relationship.

Target tutee's real-life goals: Tutees often have strong ideas on what they need help with. However, these ideas can be very short-term. Tutees might think more of getting their written homework done 'correctly' (so their teacher is not angry with them), than of really understanding the subject. Tutors have to start with the tutee's immediate concerns. But tutors should talk with tutees about their goals, encouraging them to consider wider and deeper understanding. Of course, this does not mean that tutors make tutees learn what the tutor is interested or expert in, or to think just like the tutor.

Explore understanding: Tutors need to find out what tutees already know— and what they think they know that is actually incorrect. Talking to explore deep understanding is the way to do this. Explore varied examples to make sure tutees can really use what they know in different contexts.

Small steps: Tutees often need to learn in very small steps. Do not expect them to make big leaps. Tutors often forget how long it really took them to understand something themselves.

Balance support and challenge: Tutoring is intended to be supportive—to help the tutee in the struggle to understand. But tutors should not just give tutees the right answer, or just tell or show them how to do something. This might feel helpful, but it will only result in mechanical learning without real understanding-remembering what. Understanding the process of how to find the right answer is the most important thing. So tutoring should be more than repeated drill and practice. Sometimes tutors will find that tutees have fixed ideas that are too narrow or just wrong. Then the tutor must challenge the tutees (in a gentle and helpful way), to help them loosen and then recognise and improve the quality of their thinking.

Teacher education for training and orientation of tutors is concerned with the methodology of purposeful and effective teaching. For this, tutors should come under close confidence of training institutions for teachers where teacher educators should be equipped with appropriate training programmes. Care should be taken to the following for successful implementation and follow-up of the programmes introduced:

- Tutors should be good observers of tutees' performances. There is a tendency of tutees to become passive learners and parasites. They never bother for learning in some cases but are keenly interested in getting quick success through tutors. For this reason in particular, their activities in association with their tutor's role should come under regular and sincere scanner. It should however be noted that the role of the teacher educator is not authoritative but always suggestive to both the tutor and the tutees.
- Tutors should be well-aware of the needs and priorities of the tutee. She/He should inquire into the importance of these needs and priorities from three points of view: first, how far these are contextual; second, how far these are in tune with the real purpose of learning; and third, how far these are related to the tutee's genuine urge to negotiate understanding, skill, interest, attitude and aptitude besides catering to creative and critical appreciation from time to time.
- Tutors should give importance to open-ended, short, structured assignments for the tutee in her/his speaking, reading and writing. These assignments should be periodically verified by the tutee herself/himself or by the teacher educator concerned so that these might be error-free and really reliable and stimulating to the tutee.
- For meaningful and purposeful tutoring, the tutor should encourage the tutee in the exercise of self-review. A little bit of suggestion or feedback, hints or cues verbal or non-verbal as the tutor deems apposite most often work wonders in tutoring. Even

the tutor's close association with the tutee at the time of self-review or allowance on freedom to work alone without providing guidance and supervision may sometimes pay worthy dividends.

- As tutoring is a supportive activity. The less support, the better. Otherwise, there would be a tendency of the tutee to receive some lessons from the tutor which would enable her/him to satisfy both the tutee and the concerned teacher in the institution where she/he is a student. The tutee so inspired as to be more attentive to do her/his school assignment without asking for any readymade answer from the tutor. The tutor should also be aware of the fact that some clever tutees are in the habit of manipulating the tutor by means of camouflaging or flattery. As this is a very dangerous, harmful, disturbing and indisciplined approach, stringent measures should be taken by the tutor in consultation with parents/guardians, teachers and peers of the tutee in due course of time.

One of the most embarrassing problems in tutoring is how to deal with the tutees' aggressive behaviour. Impulsive and highly prone to attention problems they develop special problems at the stage of adolescence. The tutor in some cases is at a loss how to negotiate all such problems like violence, aggression, arrogance, hooliganism etc. It is time for all concerned with education to provide a very healthy and positive climate to reduce aggressive behaviour. In this connection, the following might be very helpful for the teacher and the tutor:

> One of the best-established principles of learning is that appropriate, immediate positive consequences can make behaviour more frequent. This process is commonly called positive reinforcement. Similarly, increasing positive incentives for alternatives to problem behaviour can lead to decreases in problem behaviour. At the social level, economists' work clearly shows that changing incentives that involve money produces changes in business and societal practices. When adults provide positive consequences for a child's cooperative behaviour, non-voilent ways of handling conflict, and involvement with peers who are involved in desirable activities, they steer youth away from problem behaviour. Furthermore,

> most of the effective prevention programmes that begin when children enter school or that work with parents of aggressive children teach adults to use positive consequences systematically. By doing this, adults encourage children to develop in positive ways.
>
> Positive incentives come in many forms and can be tangible (such as money) or social (for example, praise). Additional examples of positive consequences that can increase behaviour involve giving children extra privileges and opportunities that they desire. Other consequences, such as attention from others, can be more subtle but equally powerful. Parents, teachers, other adults or peers can provide positive consequences to children. Similarly, adults and children can provide positive consequences that can help adults display more positive behaviour.[3]

Discussion plays a very important role in tutoring. The tutor herself/himself must be well-aware of the importance of tutoring. If the tutee is not in a position to be a positive partner in tutoring, the tutor should think more seriously about her/his role much ahead of the schedule of activities. There are other pre-conditions to tutoring which are as follows:

> Tutoring is greatly dependent on the stylistics of proving praise and encouragement. If the tutor knows how to praise and encourage the tutee at the right moment with right words and expressions, the purpose of tutoring is to a great extent is rewarded. She/ He should also be very particular in keeping the confidence of the tutee as high as possible and desirable. At the same time, she/he should also boost the tutee even for a minor success.
>
> Tutoring is a comprehensive endeavour to inspire the tutee in self-thinking and creativity. The tutor acts like a spark plug in enabling the tutee to think independently and ventilate the outcome of thinking in a free and lively atmosphere. This process of the exercise of thinking becomes more interesting and thrilling in the fusion of the tutor's own ability to share her/

his exercise of thinking with the tutee in a natural and spontaneous climate.

In tutoring, the suggestions and necessary pointers from teacher educators on the following might steer it towards newer direction of excellence:

Selection of relevant items,

Content validity,

Reliability,

Suggestive Qualities,

Continuity, and

Reviewing.

As regards selection of relevant items in tutoring, the tutor must take serious notes on the interest, attitude, skill and the power of appreciation of the tutee. Simultaneously, she/he should also think about the appropriate adjustment of time and other schedule of activities so that both the tutee and the tutor enjoy a very cordial and effective climate of exercise in teaching-learning.

The content validity of the assignment prepare by the tutor should be ascertained much before actual tutorial starts. Ironically, many tutors find no difference between ascertaining the selection of relevant items before tutoring and straightaway launching tutoring as they erroneously consider sheer wastage of time and energy and a useless, superfluous and repetitive exercise in the name of relevance.

How to appoint tutors? What should be the procedures of tutor recruitment? Teacher education is yet to pay attention to these and other allied serious and critical issues. On our country, several institutes if training of teachers are dealing with these issues by arranging tutorial classes. Unfortunately, in most cases, these are merely eyewash in the name of tutoring. In some cases, these arrangements of classes as tutorial activities are turned into extra regular classes.

Again, voluntary tutoring is a myth in our country. As it has more or less turned professional or semi-professional, it hardly cares for the systematic rules and regulations. Nor does it care to undergo any close relationship with teachers' training institutions. As a result, the question of responsibility in tutoring almost entirely rests on the tutors.

It is time for a conjoint and communicative endeavour between the tutor and the regular teacher to make a comprehensive and error-free and scientific programme of tutoring which would take every possible care and caution in tutoring. The teacher educators should also lend a helping hand to promote the quality of tutoring in tune with the needs and priorities of the learner-tutees. The following might be very useful for practical applications in this connection:

Specify tutoring method: Be very clear about what good tutoring would look like. Perhaps use a 'packaged' technique? Consider general or specific tutoring skills, or some of both? Structured by specific materials, or not?

Training: Train tutors and tutees together if possible. Tell them what to do. Then demonstrate what they have to do. Then give them a written and/or graphic reminder of what they have to do (to keep). Then have them immediately practise the tutoring method. Materials will be needed for practice. Observe and check whether they are doing it well. Give extra praise and coaching as needed.

Train in general tutoring skills: For example, how to establish a comfortable relationship; how to present tasks; how to give clear explanations; how to ask questions; how to demonstrate skills; how to prompt or lead tutees into imitating skills; how to check on performance; how to give feedback and praise; how to identify consistent patterns of error; how to keep progress records.

Train specific tutoring skills: As specially relevant to your tutoring method and/or materials.

Contracting: You might wish to have tutors and tutees sign some form of contract. This sets out the details of their agreement to work together.

Access to materials: These might be special materials that are specific to a tutoring programme. Or they might be regular classroom materials. Or materials publicly available (e.g., from a public library or downloaded from the internet). If tutoring is based on 'homework' set by a teacher, the school is likely to provide the materials. Sometimes the materials are specially made. They can be produced by pairs themselves, or by volunteers or administrative staff under guidance. Pairs need to be able to obtain new materials before every tutoring session. Access must be frequent, quick and easy. Does the pair know what difficulty to choose? What sequence to follow? How do they know?[4]

Autonomy is very important in learning. The tutee is a learner first and then otherwise as a tutee or in any role whatsoever. In the absence of enjoying autonomy, the tutee thinks that he has lost the joy in education. The tutor should be aware of considering the tutee's autonomy in learning in freedom and joy. She/He should also be aware that too much allowance of freedom and joy to be exercised by the tutee would defeat her purpose of tutoring. Sometimes the tutor fails to control the tutee in exercising too much freedom and joy. In that case, the whole programme of tutoring necessitates revision in the light of adjusting and incorporating newer and more exciting strategies for tutoring. The teacher educators may act as advisors in reframing the programme as the tutor desires for better tutoring.

The tutor should also take care of supervising the progress of the tutee in tutoring. She/He should create and introduce enjoyable activities for the tutee as per self-thought plans and programmes of action. She/He might consider instructions, suggestions or programmes of action in consultation with teacher educators or any other tutor on whom she/he can very well rely. It is better to avoid the practice of tutoring which remains unsupervised.

Allocation of time for tutoring is a very important factor in tutoring. Tutoring is neither a second and secondary affair. It is an inseparable part of education in general and teacher education in particular. Therefore, in framing the time table for tutoring, a comprehensive, integral, complementary and careful approach to advancement in teaching-learning should be prioritised. Suggestions from parents and guardians should also be invited and introduced in tutoring with certain positive modifications as the tutor thinks best for the tutee.

Appropriate stage specific preparation of tutors has now become very important. The tutors should have a sound knowledge of the society to which the tutee belongs. A little addition and/or alteration of the programme of tutoring in tune with changing needs and priorities of the society brings forth variety and progress in tutoring. In this connection, the role of the teacher educators in re-defining and re-enlivening tutoring is undeniable.

The need for specially qualified tutors is also to be seriously considered. As mentioned earlier, the role, the tutor and tutoring for refinement of tutee-progress is yet to be given its proper worth. Unless our mind-sets are changed, tutoring would remain a thankless and secondary affair in education for teaching, training, orientation and excellence.

To make the curriculum less textbook centred and more learner-thinking and learner-specific, tutoring will have to significantly contribute at every stage of education. Teacher education should, therefore, prepare tutors along with freshers, teacher-students or trainee teachers. The need has, of late, been aggravated with many issues where the role of the tutor and tutoring has opened a challenging dimension. Needless to say, the issues related to tutoring and related affairs will have to be addressed with an altogether radical mind-set as a viable means of education and orientation of tutors along with teacher preparation. As the National Curriculum Framework for Teacher Education (NCFTE) characteristically suggests:

> There is now a public acknowledgement that the current system of schooling imposes tremendous burden on our children. This burden arises from an incoherent curriculum structure that is often dissociated from the personal and social milieu of children as also from the inadequate preparation of teachers who are unable to make connections with children and respond to their needs in imaginative ways. Teachers need to be creators of knowledge and thinking professionals. They need to be empowered to recognise and value what children

> learn from their home, social and cultural environment and to create opportunities for children to discover, learn and develop. The recommendations of the NCF on school curriculum are built on this plank. Educationists are also of the view that the burden arises from treating knowledge as a 'given', as an external reality existing outside the learner and embedded in textbooks.
>
> This view of education points to the need to take a fresh look at teacher preparation. Education is not a mechanical activity of information transmission and teachers are not information dispensers. Teachers need to be looked as crucial mediating agents through whom curriculum is transacted and knowledge is co-constructed along with learners. Textbooks by themselves do not help in developing knowledge and understanding. Learning is not confined to the four walls in the classroom. For this to happen, there is a need to connect knowledge to life outside the school and enrich the curriculum by making it less textbook centred.[5]

A new dawn of awareness in making tutoring meaningful, purposeful, dynamic, interesting and enlivening in education and teaching is long overdue in teacher education in the twenty-first century. Tutoring is neither a substitute nor an additional activity. It is also teaching—genuine, ardent, sincere, serious and challenging. It is also promising and reflective, creative and innovative. It should no longer be treated as a mere curative exercise. Indeed, it is a far more in-depth endeavour to explore the undiscovered arena of learning the child for quality teaching and excellent efflorescence of personality.

Let the tutor be allowed to enrich tutoring with maximum effectiveness. Let her/him show new pathways to introduce ideas from a new angle of quality acceleration. The following suggestions for practical applications in tutoring are very significant:

Goals of monitoring: Seek to detect and solve any problems before they become large; find opportunities to give plentiful praise and show enthusiasm to keep motivation high; ensure the tutoring technique does not show signs of 'drift'; check that pairs are maintaining positive social relationships; be sure that materials used are from an appropriate sequence/ level of difficulty; and generally review the complexity and richness of the learning taking place.

Self-help guide: Make a simple self-help guide of common problems in tutoring with suggestions about how these might be solved. You will keep adding to this. With 'packaged' techniques, clues about likely problems will be found in the literature.

Self-referral: Let tutors and tutees know it is usual for many pairs to encounter some temporary difficulty, so this is not the fault of either helper or helped. They should know who to ask if one or both have any difficulty (with a particular problem, the tutoring technique or each other). They could seek help from other pairs before approaching a teacher.

Self-recording: The pair should record their progress, and a monitoring teacher or a tutoring organiser can then check these records or diaries from time to time.

Discussion: Talk with the tutors and tutees about how things are going, perhaps at 'planning' or ' debriefing' meetings. You might do this individually or in groups, with tutors and tutees together or separate.

Direct observation: Carefully observe tutoring as it happens. (Do not assume that even the most intelligent tutor will be aware if they are going wrong). A checklist of the elements of the tutoring technique will be helpful to structure these observations consistently. You could also ask 'spare' tutors to monitor sometimes, using this checklist. It is possible to use video or audio recording for monitoring, and this can be useful for feedback to individual pairs or the group as a whole, as well as being valuable as a training aid for subsequent projects.[6]

Tutoring can very well be amalgamated with teaching provided that the identity and purpose are not doled out in the whirlwind of re-framing the curriculum framework. Special attention should be given to training and orientation of tutors on diverse issues related to the following:

(a) time table,

(b) formation of pair-work schedule,

(c) use of library and ICT,

(d) review programmes,

(e) organisational and administrative guidelines,

(f) guidance and supervision check-list.

The above is not a permanent and obligatory one but simply suggestive. One can add or omit any point which seems to be ineffective due to unavoidable reasons. On the whole, however, tutoring calls forth care and attention in accordance with the changing situation.

Who ignores tutoring as a marvellous exercise in teacher education?

References

1. Topping, K: *Tutoring,* International Bureau of Education, UNESCO, 1997, pp. 6-7.
2. *Ibid.,* pp. 9-10.
3. Foster, S.L. *et al: Preventing Behaviour Problems: What Works,* International Bureau of Education, UNESCO, 2002, p. 10.
4. Topping, K.: *Tutoring, International Bureau of Education,* UNESCO, 1997, pp. 26-27.
5. *National Curriculum Framework for Teacher Education: Towards Preparing Professional and Humane Teacher,* National Council for Teacher Education, New Delhi, 2009, p. 4.
6. Topping, K.: *Tutoring,* International Bureau of Education, UNESCO, 1997, pp. 28-29.

13 Postscript

The quest for an ideal teacher is never-ending and alluring. It is a quest that promises new horizons of teaching-learning, excellence and advancement, quality and ascent. It prepares an altogether new platform in the altar of teaching-learning. It encourages a new beginning of devotion to self-realisation and self-development in and through education at the cathedral of consciousness for excellence in every direction.

What type of a teacher do we want to encounter in educational institutions? What ought to be her/his duties and responsibilities for the advancement of learning? Here is an excellent pointer:

> During recent years so much stress has been laid on 'research' and 'original work' that the primary function and duty of a teacher are in danger of being overlooked, it seems that every teacher must, else sinning greatly, be a researcher; that he must have done 'original work'; that he must have published some book or papers. Public opinion demands 'productive scholarship'. A specialist has been defined as a man who knows more and more about less and less. Work of real originality deserves to be admired and encouraged. Every facility must be given in the way of apparatus, journals, and a well-equipped library. Liberal grants must be made for sending

> out expeditions. But the university is not merely a place of research. Its membership consists for the most part of undergraduates, who have to learn the art of living. The teacher's main concern must be the student and his growth; he must be an inspiration to his pupils; he must mould their character; he must be a living influence for them. He must possess a quickness of sympathy and breadth of outlook and understanding. He must shape them not merely by the training of the intellect but by the discipline of spirit. What can give more joy than the consciousness that one has contributed to the maturing and shaping of a character, to the equipment of an intellect, to the enlargement and widening of a vision? Constant contact with the pupil, sharing in his life, enjoying his fullest confidence, providing him with opportunities for the cultivation of his taste, these, and the imparting of knowledge, the study are the teacher's main duty; these are also his privilege and a source of unending satisfaction and delight. In order that he should succeed, he must be a person of high character; nothing that he says or does should fall below a certain moral standard. Spirits full of activity and full of energy that are pressing forward, eagerly, hopefully, rushing onward to fine issues, must be touched only by what is elevating and ennobling.[1]

A good teacher knows how to adjust herself/himself to undesirable teaching-learning atmosphere. She/he knows how to feel at home in teaching under constraints like overcrowded classrooms and disturbances outside or inside the classrooms. As Professor Highet points out:

> Every profession has its atmosphere, its setting, and those who practise it must feel at home there. It is silly to become an actor if you want a settled home and time to think. Do not enter journalism unless you like the bustle of a large noisy office, welcome travel and the unexpected, and hope to like it all the rest of your life. If you do not enjoy the prospect of facing the young in large groups, if you would always prefer working in a laboratory or reading in a library, you will never be a good teacher.

> Of course nobody can bear young people all the time. One of the pleasures and necessities of the teacher's life is to escape—into a cool library or a little garden—away from their noise and their devilish energy. Among the most difficult jobs in the profession are those which give very little respite and condemn the dean to be always on call, the house-master to spend every day of his working life among the boys. Still, these jobs are not thrust upon us, but taken by choice. Those who hold them usually relish them. Remember, you must not armour yourself against the energies of the young. You must not be the policeman watching the mob. You must be the leader of a group—something higher than the actor with his audience, something lower than the priest with his congregation, something kindlier than the officer with his unit. You must always feel what the orator feels when he addresses an audience partly friendly and partly docile, and senses after a little that they are with him. Such a man is borne upwards and swept onwards by energy which flows into him from outside, from the group of which he is the heart and the voice. The good teacher feels that same flow of energy, constantly supplied by the young. If he can canalise it, he will never be tired. At least, not while he is teaching.[2]

Redesigning teacher education for quality and excellence in teaching is subject to the responses received from the teacher concerned. It may at the outset be admitted that unless the teacher gives positive responses to different teaching strategies formulated for better teaching, it is absolutely meaningless for the purpose to be aimed at under any teaching-learning climate.

Is the teacher aware of her/his own position in terms of adequacy? Does she/he really ponder over the problems of the learners in learning a lesson? Does she/he take note of the answers from the students, which require a little bit of addition or alteration to be made in a conjoint and endearing ambience of teaching-learning? These and similar other queries must haunt a conscientious teacher in the method of teaching:

One of the sharpest worries of a conscientious teacher is his own inadequacy. He has not made this vital point clear. Did they really understand his sketch of that theory, and his refutation of it? Should he have given more time to the first half of the programme? These worries can be removed, or at least mitigated, by three or four hours saved at the end of the term for revising the course, filling in the gaps, and re-emphasising the important points. It is tempting sometimes to end a lecture-course with a rousing peroration on the final topic, but its impression soon fades, whereas a steady, cool, clear review of the entire ground will, in a comparatively short time and with comparatively little effort, make a far deeper and more lasting mark on these flexible minds.

As the class retraces its journey, it will have a fine opportunity to ask questions, and you to prompt them and answer them. Never underestimate the power of a well-put question to illuminate the darkness. Students who have been passively absorbing informations and allowing it to trickle out almost as fast as it was poured in will often come to life and take an active interest in their work when questions start flying. But the real value of the question-period at the end is for the conscientious students it is worthwhile to read through a lecture-notebook kept by a student of good intelligence and industry. The gaps and misunderstandings in it will astound you. Often these youngsters are afraid to ask you to fill in the gaps, because they do not want to give themselves away. They think you will snub them, or answer perfunctorily. If you do, you are committing a crime. Instead, you should make it easy for them to ask for corrections, full names, the exact figures, the complete references. Don't simply wait for them to demand help. Offer it. You have not always spoken clearly. Foreign names and complex formulas are difficult to write down quickly. A cough will cover up half a vital silence; and, in many cities nowadays, at least five minutes of every hour's teaching is made inaudible by the roar of transport aircraft apparently flying just above the roofs. The last few meetings of the class are your

> opportunity to wash away all that mud, and reveal your own lost pearls.[3]

What, then, about the role of the teacher in imparting total education? Are the learners coming under this fold right now? If not, are we aware that it is the crisis of all crisis in teacher education? Are we in a position to prepare our teachers to be justified to our learners for cultivation of total education? Indeed, we need a new horizon in teacher education enriched in new understanding, new prospects, new priorities, new ventures and new visions of poignancy and perfection, fullness and devotion:

> Most people would agree that we are passing through a crisis, be it a crisis of civilisation or, as some fear, of evolution, or both. But as to the nature of the crisis, its causes and cure, the doctors are not agreed. In spite of the split among specialists, it is a safe guess that in order to meet the challenge, we shall need a new strategy or a new understanding. Ultimately, all failure of action is a failure of thought. Briefly, we shall need a new theory and practice of education. It will be education in a new key, what we may call Total or Integral Education. Unfortunately, for some minds the phrase has acquired awful associations. They confuse it with Totalitarianism's violent experiment with untruth. What Herr Hitler and his stooges were trying to do was to throttle human growth and freedom, in the name of the almighty State. Total education, one might say, is the exact opposite of what the Hitlers have tried to do. It is education for fullness and freedom. Total education is part of our predicament—for it involves difficult and delicate adjustments—as well as the way out, if there is a way out. No patchwork, patchwork conceptions and piecemeal practice, will do. With regard to the education of children—and where education is concerned, we are little better than children—it has been said that we must introduce the child to himself. It must be the same with total education, which will introduce man to himself, to the whole of relationships and purposes in terms of which man defines or creates himself. In the divided world today, total education or education of the whole man is clearly 'an obligation imposed by the nature of things; a

> mission in which every man or woman who knows the difference between true and false, between what has a right to be and what has not, is called to be teacher and learner both in one'. In our present peril, total education is the summary imperative which we must obey, or be damned for disobeying.
>
> Essentially a social institution or enterprise, education is concerned very often in an unconscious and haphazard fashion, with the transmission of skills and values, with know-why no less than know-how. Some idea, vague or clear, right or wrong, of purpose and personality, some aim of life is implicit in education anywhere and everywhere. But most, if not all, historical cultures have been obliged to work within a narrow range of limited ideas, limited by rigid, regional, or time-barred notions, and they have been ultimately destroyed by corrosive conflicts and contradictions. Everywhere, some aspect or capacity or manner of adjustment has dominated. A full and happy flowering of the human personality, of all its possibilities, has been rarely attempted, much less achieved. In the existentialist phrase, we are all broken mirrors. The idea of wholeness, with which is connected the idea of holiness, has not been the chief aim of most education or of civilisations. Some kind of functional efficiency and for the rest a well-adjusted individual is all that most cultures have cared for. But, today, the physical drawing together of the world and our common destiny have forced upon us a common approach to the problem of education. We need a philosophy of total or world education.[4]

The exploration, enrichment and expansion of a new horizon of teacher education from the perspective of total education as above is long overdue. While global civilisation and culture are suffering from the absence of right education with right mission and vision, teacher education in our country looks forward to rethinking the role of the teacher under an abnormally socio-cultural and socio-aesthetic ukase. Lost is the paradise of teaching and teacher education where teaching is more than a serene and disciplined activity where the ultimate goal is to enjoy 'calmness of mind, all passions spent' in pursuit of the fullness of life and the beyond, and add the learning an endless devotion in the cathedral of consciousness for purity of the mind, kindliness and magnanimity of the heart, and self-realisation and self-sacrifice for the society. Lost, too, is the paradise in the hallowed name of educational institutions—the altar of awareness as they ought to be anywhere and everywhere in the pursuit of teaching-learning—which are nowadays victims of perilous circumstances writ large in violence, bloodshed and even loss of life. In fact, teaching is, we are afraid, not either a mere profession or a matter-of-fact vocation but a poignant promise for the full flowering of perfection in every altruistic aspect of humane enlightenment.

The canvas of teaching, especially teaching children is so vast and rapidly changing that the twenty first century teacher ought to be well-informed and equipped with the latest trends and strategies as well-suited to the children's diverse attitudes, interests, aptitudes and appreciations to different branches of knowledge and experiences, motivational areas and queries. As a rationale to learner studies on childhood, child, and adolescent development and learning, the role of the teacher in developing the foundations of learning for children as suggested by the NCTE is very significant:

> The courses on Learner Studies are visualised as the first systematic introduction to the study of childhood, child development and adolescence. Beginning teachers need to engage with and understand *children of different ages* by interacting with them and observing them in diverse social, economic and cultural contexts rather than through an exclusive focus on psychological theories of child development. This would include a close study of *adolescence* in contemporary India as it poses several new challenges that emerge from the personal as well as social turmoil characteristic of societies in transition. It is equally important for teachers to engage with the *social construct of childhood and adolescence,* the various socio-cultural and political dimensions associated with its positioning and development in society.
>
> Foundational learning in this area involves establishing links between developmental constructs and principles in

psychological theory and the larger socio-political realities in which children grow and develop. Understanding the development of children is diverse contexts is necessary to equip student teachers to address diversity in the classroom and to teach within the frame of inclusive education. Pre-service teacher education programmes at all levels (including senior secondary) should be designed to include the observation and study of young children in order to appreciate the developmental process as a continuum.

An adequate opportunity for this can be provided through courses designed around key concepts and research from the disciplines of Psychology, Philosophy as well as Sociology.

Understanding children's (of diverse age groups) questions, their observations of natural and social phenomena; *enquiring into children's thinking and learning* and learning to listen to children with attention and empathy are necessary pre-requisites to develop teachers who are learner sensitive. Such engagement will help teachers to understand that learning is not a linear process; that it is a divergent process, essentially spiral in nature, and takes place in a variety of situations, including everyday contexts. Exclusive engagement with theories of learning fails to provide this perspective.

Every child needs to be made aware of the importance of healthy living and preventing disease. This is an urgent need, therefore, to generate health awareness and cultivate habits conducive to healthy living. It is suggested that comprehensive, systematic and scientific approaches to health education and health awareness be included in teacher education curricula. The contents proposed include: nutrition, personal and environmental hygiene, family and *school health,* disease prevention and control including HIV/AIDS, mental health, prevention of accidents, health information, use of health services, *physical health and sports.*[5]

In the professional development of teachers, all the areas of proficiencies under teacher education cannot be assessed in terms of certain rules and regulations to be strictly followed. Teaching is never prescriptive but innovative where the teacher knows best how to be true to and successful in teaching. Teaching cannot but be essentially arresting and inspiring, poignant and interesting.

Contrary to the usual methods and strategies of teaching, a thought-provoking and penetrating teacher cautiously enters into the learner's world of curiosity and interest and becomes successful in stimulating the latter abundantly. The human mind has the infinite capacity to unfold the unknown and the undiscovered world of knowledge and wisdom, mystery and imagination. It is the task of the teacher to ignite and illumine the latter by means of extending a warm welcome to the latter in the efflorescence of learning. As Professor Highet characteristically spells out:

> We know the minimum diet which will keep a child alive. We know the maximum quantity of food he can absorb. But no one knows, no one can even guess how much knowledge a child will want and, if it is presented to him in the right way, will digest. Therefore, it is simply useless to teach a child even the elements of a subject, without being prepared to answer his questions about the upper ranges and the inner depths of the subject. And from the teacher's point of view it is far more difficult to do so. A limited field of material stirs very few imaginations. It can be learnt off by heart, but seldom creatively understood and never loved. A subject that carries the mind out in limitless journeys will, if it is well-taught, make the learner eager to master all the preliminary essentials and press on.
>
> Young people hate grown-ups for many reasons. One of the reasons is that they feel grown-ups minds are fixed and limited. Whenever they meet a man or a woman who does not always say what they expect, who tells them novel stories about strange aspects of the world, who throws unexpected lights on what they sadly know as ordinary dull life, who seems as completely alive, sensitive, energetic, and zestful as they themselves, they usually admire him or her. It is true that we cannot all be fountains of energy and novelty throughout every day, but we ought, if we are teachers, to be so keen on

> our own subjects that we can talk interestingly about unusual aspects of them to young people who would otherwise have been dully neutral, or—worse—eagerly disappointed. A teacher must believe in the value and interest of his subject as a doctor believes in health.
>
> The neglect of this principle is one of the chief reasons for the bad teaching that makes pupils hate schools and universities and turn away from valuable fields of knowledge.[6]

Another very radical and distinctive horizon in teacher education is the departure from existing sham values in life and society. The teacher is neither an analyser nor a synthesiser in the teaching of values that ultimately bring forth confusions worst confounded in ignorance and ignominy. She/He always welcomes fresh thoughts and ideas received from buoyant learners who love 'revision or modification of the present as well as ancient ideals and practices':

> Extreme specialisation, knowing more and more about less and less, the logical end of the analytical approach, carries its own danger. Also, the overall commercialism of the age has to submit to more human purposes; the era of competition has to yield to the idea of welfare and mutual aid. The impersonality of science and organisation has to be set right by a new idea of personality and inter-personal relationships. Men are not equations or figures in statistics. The dichotomy of knowledge and wisdom must be got rid of. Dogmas of every kind, religious and scientific, have to be replaced by a more liberal attitude towards truth; it will not be *either/or,* but both. It must not be science versus spirituality, but science and spirituality, spirituality as the science of unity, *ekavidya.* Instead of part, or specialised, education, education for the particular jobs or functions, we shall need 'the co-education of both body and mind'. There is a wisdom of the body which the wise have always known and respected. This will be something more than physical culture or gymnastics. One of its results will be to end the isolation of action from contemplation. In *The Future of Education* Livingstone has pointed out: We lead a

> life of action without thought: or we think in a vacuum, without the realities and problems of the world. Neither form of isolation is satisfactory.' For all this to happen, we shall need new loyalties; and instead of regimentation, or the narrow view, we shall follow freedom, whatever the risk. It is needless to say that the militant nationalist formula will have to be replaced by a growing international idea. The obsession with parochial histories has to give place to a saner philosophy of universal history. As Arnold Toynbee has said: "The peoples of the world cannot learn to understand each other, if they confine their attention to the present surface of life and ignore the historical depths," it is out of historical necessity that we must change our ways, and educate ourselves anew.[7]

Are the new horizons of teacher education abloom with this promise? If not, when, O when!

References

1. Jha, Amarnath: "The Meaning of University Education", Quoted from, *An Anthology of Modern Indian Eloquence,* Eds. K.M. Munshi and R.R. Diwakar, Bharatiya Vidya Bhavan, Mumbai, 1960, pp. 250-251.
2. Highet, Gilbert: *The Art of Teaching,* Methuen and Company Limited, London, 1963, pp. 26-27.
3. *Ibid.,* pp. 148-149.
4. Ghose, Sisirkumar: "Total Education", *Crisis of Crisis,* Bharatiya Vidya Bhavan, Mumbai, 1972, pp. 37-38.
5. *National Curriculum Framework for Teacher Education: Towards Preparing Professional and Humane Teacher,* National Council for Teacher Education, New Delhi, 2009, pp. 28-29.
6. Highet, Gilbert: *The Art of Teaching,* Methuen and Company Limited, London, 1963, 13-14.
7. Ghose, Sisir Kumar: *Ibid.,* pp. 39-40.

Index